The European Union–Maghrebian Dialogues

Echoes of Disappointments Past

Author

William H. Lewis

January 2001

About CSIS

The Center for Strategic and International Studies (CSIS), established in 1962, is a private, tax-exempt institution focusing on international public policy issues. Its research is nonpartisan and nonproprietary.

CSIS is dedicated to policy impact. It seeks to inform and shape selected policy decisions in government and the private sector to meet the increasingly complex and difficult global challenges that leaders will confront in this new century. It achieves this mission in four ways: by generating strategic analysis that is anticipatory and interdisciplinary; by convening policymakers and other influential parties to assess key issues; by building structures for policy action; and by developing leaders.

CSIS does not take specific public policy positions. Accordingly, all views, positions, and conclusions expressed in this publication should be understood to be solely those of the author.

President and Chief Executive Officer: John J. Hamre
Senior Vice President and Director of Studies: Erik R. Peterson
Director of Publications: James R. Dunton

Library of Congress Cataloging-in-Publication Data
CIP information available on request.

The CSIS Press
Center for Strategic and International Studies
1800 K Street, N.W., Washington, D.C. 20006
Telephone: (202) 887-0200
Fax: (202) 775-3199
E-mail: books@csis.org
Web site: http://www.csis.org/

Contents

Preface   iv

Acknowledgments   viii

1. Introduction   1

2. The Basic Template of Ties   6

3. The Travails of Morocco   17

4. The Way Elsewhere—Algeria   23

5. Tunisia—Opportunities Found, Opportunities Misplaced   31

6. Horizons Near and Far   36

7. The United States—A Partner or a Marginal Actor?   39

Appendix.   Barcelona Declaration Adopted at the Euro-
             Mediterranean Conference   43

About the Author   63

Preface

THE DEMISE OF THE COLD WAR IN 1989 led governments in Western Europe to turn their attention to regional organizations and institutions that might require strengthening in order to meet two basic objectives—maintenance of stability and economic growth in Europe, and protection of security interests in adjacent geographic regions. In an examination of security issues in 1991, Jacques Delors, then president of the European Commission, identified Western Europe's southern flank as a region of paramount interest to the states that would shortly comprise the core membership of the emerging European Union (EU). Several years later, Willy Claes, then secretary general of the North Atlantic Treaty Organization (NATO), urged an examination of newly emerged security threats in the Mediterranean basin and, in the process, identified Islamic fundamentalism as the principal source of instability in the region. Confronted with public criticism for his remarks, Claes was forced to retract what was widely viewed as a naïve and unsupportable statement.

The European Union (EU), for its part, put forth a more sophisticated assessment, turning away from traditional Cold War precepts of deterrence and containment. The EU approach assumed a basic linkage of Mediterranean instability with the economic, social, and political problems confronting governments in the region. Meeting at Barcelona, Spain, with representative delegations from North Africa and the Middle East in the latter half of 1995, the EU proposed a special partnership be formed, one in which the Union would assist in the creation by 2010 of a free trade zone, embracing 30 to 40 countries and 800 million people.

The EU also proposed a multidimensional approach to enhance stability. The 26-page declaration agreed to at Barcelona contained three main "baskets," or goals:

- Adoption of political partnership principles (e.g., respect for international law, democracy, and the rule of law by governing institutions);

- Economic partnership, including reduction of tariff barriers, and enlarged financial and economic assistance to southern Mediterranean participants; and

- Partnership in cultural, social, and human affairs.

Morocco, Algeria, and Tunisia were represented at Barcelona and fully endorsed the declaration in expectation of special entitlements given their long-standing ties with the EU's predecessor, the European Community. The economic basket seemed especially attractive because it appeared to suggest that EU tariff barriers impeding North African agricultural exports would end and support for government investment and industrial expansion would be assured. Over the long term, a Euro-Mediterranean economic area (EMEA) would sustain North Africa (Maghreb) governments in efforts to participate in processes of globalization and to become beneficiaries of the technological revolution then unfolding.

A central element in this study is an understanding of the reasons why hopes and expectations aroused at Barcelona have not been met in any of the three baskets fashioned. Early indication of a troubled future became apparent in the political realm. The declared objective was to encourage strengthening of democratic institutions and good governance in the Maghreb and elsewhere along the southern Mediterranean littoral. Included as precepts were respect for human rights, law and order, and freedom of expression as a means to protect against instability and political extremism.

For the Maghreb's ruling elite, there was little enthusiasm for far-reaching political experimentation out of fear that liberalization would undermine the legitimacy of governing institutions and erode the foundations of the state. In the view of the elite, security of the state and its national institutions was of primordial importance given early indications that the EU was not prepared to provide economic and social safety nets for political reforms envisioned in the Barcelona Declaration.

To deal with economic needs, the EU proposed to make 5.5 billion ecu available over the initial five-year period (1995–2000) of the Barcelona partnership. This figure was subsequently reduced owing to growing demands for economic assistance for East European applicants for EU membership—which has been denied to the Maghreb in states. Crises in the Balkans following the breakup of the Yugoslav Federation (1990–present) have added to the EU's contractual obligations. These include several billion dollars in a preaccession set-aside for Bulgaria and Romania over the 2000–2006 period and a pledge in excess of $10 billion for reconstruction and humanitarian assistance to Southeast Europe over a comparable period. The EU has been the largest aid donor to five Balkan countries as part of its Stability and Association Program. The impact for the Maghrebian states has been a sense of donor fatigue reflected in aid shortfalls and failure to implement joint projects.

Recognizing the widening Maghrebian dissatisfaction, the union's Brussels bureaucracy has encouraged France, Spain, and Italy to compensate for EU shortfalls with bilateral economic support programs for each of the Maghrebian states. This compensatory approach would appear a natural evolution of historical, economic, and cultural ties extant between the Maghreb and Southern Europe's union members. The approach reflects the natural divide of the members, with Germany directing its attention to Russia and Eastern Europe, with the Scandinavians attaching special importance to the former Soviet Baltic republics, and with the United Kingdom directing its principal policy interests and goals toward the eastern Mediterranean–Persian Gulf regions, in close collaboration with the United States.

The bilateral strategy has a certain symmetry and elegance of design. In part, it meets Europe's oil and natural gas requirements (one-fourth of energy imports emanate from Algeria and Libya) while it provides export revenues for North Africa. Second, the strategy enhances the bargaining position of France, Spain, and Italy over associate status countries such as Morocco and Tunisia—as was evidenced in the recent agreement over fishing rights between Morocco and Spain that resulted in major concessions by Rabat in the face of combined EU pressures. Morocco and Tunisia are disadvantaged by their ongoing dependence on France and Spain as intercessors and advocates for Maghrebian interests in EU councils. Finally, the EU retains paramountcy of position with respect to "measures equivalent to quantitative trade restrictions"—a controversial issue, subject to interpretation by the European Court of Justice. This complex issue deals with restrictions resulting from differing technical and regulatory standards that discriminate on the basis of place of production, for example, import tariffs on German hair dryers that fail to meet Moroccan standards favoring its local manufacturers.

The third Barcelona basket, harmonization of cultural and social interests, has proved difficult to implement. At the heart of the problem is the Maghrebian belief that the EU ultimately intends homogenization of European and Arab-Moslem cultures. In such circumstances, Arab-Moslem societies will confront an existential challenge—preservation of traditional values and cultural identity or surrender. The more skeptical Maghrebians observe that EU Europe has little to offer in the social and economic realms to compensate for any surrender that occurs. They point to the hesitancy with which the European governments greet proposals and abandon restrictive immigration policies—characterized as a fortress-Europe stance—to lessen demographic and societal pressures currently confronting Maghrebian countries. The skeptics complain that, fearful of cultural contamination, Europeans open the wall of containment from time to time only to admit for brief periods farm workers and other unskilled labor.

A further weakness in efforts to produce a well-constructed third basket was revealed during the EU summit held in Lisbon in the spring of 2000 when France's representative acknowledged that the union had failed to develop a "European social model," incorporating growth, employment, and social interests. Further, no credible database had been established to chart population movements, labor shortfalls, violations of human rights, or discriminatory acts against foreigners resident in EU member countries. France, holding the six-month EU presidency that began officially in July 2000, intended to urge several initiatives to establish effective common social programs over the next several years. Whatever the ultimate destination of French initiatives, they will have little immediate impact on EU-Maghreb relations. While degrading the importance of the third basket, European policy makers will retain as a central goal a preventive effort against political instability in North Africa and other southern Mediterranean countries.

The sense of urgency that seized EU thinking about the Maghreb early in the 1990s has abated perceptibly. Morocco's transition from the 30-year rule of King Hassan to his youthful son, Muhammad, has been negotiated without undue strain, and some effort is being made to reinvigorate the national economy. President Bouteflika of Algeria, despite some public relations excesses, has succeeded in reducing the level of violence that has blighted Algeria during the 1990s and, most notably, has secured the disbandment of the largest insurgent force, the AIS. Nevertheless, the militancy continues to dominate government decision making. Tunisia, under the firm direction of President Ben Ali, has registered impressive economic development gains that, in turn, have benefited an emergent middle class. Overall, early 1990s European fears of a radical Islamist tidal wave have abated, and trading ties with Arab participants in the Barcelona partnership show signs of modest growth.

Maghrebian-Southern European codependency is likely to remain in place despite occasional frictions, but the EU, in the overall, is unlikely to register significant gains over the next half decade in securing Maghrebian support for the Barcelona processes. The basis for this assessment will be outlined in the pages that follow. What remains clear is France's continuing central role as lynchpin in sustaining the North–South relationship. However, the future configuration of political authority in the Maghreb will be centered in its ruling classes. Each has its own center gravity and distinctive character—the monarchy in Morocco, *le pouvoir* in Algeria, and an unabashed autocrat in Tunisia. The EU, facing decision-making-system overload, can play only a marginal role in seeking to facilitate processes of political change and economic reform in the Maghreb.

Acknowledgments

The author and CSIS gratefully acknowledge the support received for this study from the U.S. Institute of Peace in Washington, D.C., and the Earhart Foundation in Ann Arbor, Michigan. The assistance rendered to the author by the Middle East Institute also proved invaluable.

CHAPTER 1

Introduction

Tʜᴇ ᴇᴜʀᴏᴘᴇᴀɴ ᴜɴɪᴏɴ (ᴇᴜ) ɪs ᴇᴍʙᴀʀᴋᴇᴅ ᴏɴ ᴀ ʜɪsᴛᴏʀɪᴄ ᴊᴏᴜʀɴᴇʏ, one that will shape the political and economic landscape of Europe for decades to come. Romano Prodi, the current union commissioner—the self-described European prime minister—suggests somewhat grandiosely that the EU will have fashioned a "common European soul" by the year 2007. Other EU officials, in more earthbound terms, merely hope that the union will create a common economic and political identity that, in turn, will add immeasurably to the continent's strategic weight in a period of globalization and revolutionary technological change. Such hopes and expectations disguise the fact that the union, since the founding Treaty of Rome, has always remained an institutional work in progress.

Institutional Reform

EU growth and development over the past quarter century have been attended by wide-ranging uncertainties reflecting divergent goals and aspirations of the union's founders. Many of the issues that confronted them during the institution's formative period still await resolution in the new millennium: What standards and precepts will guide the union as it confronts simultaneous challenges to widen EU membership and deepen existing institutional foundations? What institutional reforms must be addressed? At the national level, what prerogatives and cultural values should be preserved or surrendered? Can the 15 members and applicants for membership fashion agreed foreign and national security goals?

Existing imponderables are many, and EU leadership decision making appears becalmed. The hope in Brussels is for a Europe of enhanced economic weight and political capacity. The hope in London is for pragmatic progress on carefully selected issues instead of adoption of grand designs and spectacular leaps into the unknown. Most EU members have adopted a reserved posture on these and related questions. Implicit is an awareness that Europe must fashion its own security policies in order to reduce dependence on the U.S. strategic military umbrella.

Clearly, the EU faces a daunting decision-making agenda. Its unprecedented nature was outlined recently by Simon Serfaty, a European affairs specialist:

> What makes this agenda unprecedented is that all questions are faced simultaneously, notwithstanding the enormity of the task. What makes the coming years, when this agenda must be addressed, a defining moment is the implicit (and valid) assumption that failure to move effectively in any one area might compromise the others: deepen in order to widen, widen in order to deepen, and reform in order to do both. Finally, the defining moment is made some-

what unique by the relative predictability of its calendar...one and probably two IGCs to reform EU institutions with new treaties, in December 2000 and again in 2004–2005; a single European currency for all 15 EU states...by 2002–2003, to complete the single market and face a broad range of unintentional fiscal consequences; admission of many new members as of 2005 and for the balance of the decade, however membership has been redefined through the earlier IGCs; and much more.[1]

Enlargement

As decisions on institutional reform of the EU are taken, the question of enlargement (from 15 to 30 members) looms as an imposing overhang.[2] The more impatient candidates for accession (Poland and Hungary) have expressed dismay as deadlines are lengthened and, in their view, the bar for admission appears to be constantly rising. After two years of negotiation, a number of controversial issues remain to be resolved, including free movement of people, budgetary allocations, enhanced border security, and import restrictions and subsidies for agricultural products. For Germany and Austria, the main issue is controlled movement of people; for France it is border security and maintenance of agricultural subsidies; and for Spain the primary objective is preservation of its large share of EU regional aid. The Scandinavian EU member states are fixated on the accession issue. They believe that special consideration should be accorded the Baltic states of Estonia and Lithuania; Germany favors Slovenia; France urges that Romania's credentials be accorded special weight. Given the lack of consensus, EU accession is not likely to occur before 2005 at the earliest.

Constitution

Pressed by a welter of issues, the EU's leading powers, Germany and France, appear in doubt as to institutional reforms that should be addressed or strategies to adopt with respect to fashioning a constitution. The union's central institution, the European Commission, which is both its civil service (with more than 15,000 bureaucrats) and the its leading policyminder, is of little help. It was riven by scandal in 1999. Many national governments now question the commission's aims, methods, and "value for money," believing it forfeited a great deal of credibility when charges of corruption were substantiated, forcing the resignation of its commissioners at year's end.

Mediterranean Partnership

In the midst of this uncertainty, the EU leadership persists in efforts to cast a wide economic and political net encompassing nations situated along the southern shores of the Mediterranean basin. The concept of a Euro-Mediterranean partnership (EMP) was first approved by the EU and 12 attending southern Mediterranean

---

1. Simon Serfaty (statement before the Committee on International Relations, U.S. House of Representatives, Washington, D.C., November 10, 1999).

2. *The Economist*, June 6, 2000, 8.

states at the EU's Barcelona Conference held on November 27–28, 1995. The conference's avowed aim was the creation of a Euro-Mediterranean free trade area, one in which the EU pledged substantial financial support for southern Mediterranean countries. The EU also proposed to launch political dialogues with these states, the ultimate purpose being to spur the growth of internal democracy within southern Mediterranean countries and encourage peaceful resolution of their disputes. These general objectives were spelled out in the Barcelona Declaration (see the appendix). To facilitate efforts at goal achievement, the EU early on offered ongoing consultation and aid to its southern basin partners. Mediterranean aid programs have since become a shambles, however, according to a recent report issued by Chris Patten, the EU commissioner for external relations. In mid-2000, Patten announced that union promises to southern partners had clearly exceeded union capabilities and were in partial default. Indeed, should the union cease current efforts to organize new aid schemes, the organization would require at minimum an additional nine years, at current rates of expenditure, to meet its previous pledged obligations to its southern Mediterranean partners.

Euro-Mediterranean partnership is not a program conducted in watertight compartments separated from bilateral European relationships with southern Mediterranean partners. North Africa's Maghrebian states—Morocco, Algeria, and Tunisia—bulk large in the ruling circles of Paris, Madrid, and Rome, especially when the specter of political instability in the Maghreb threatens access to its proximate, available, and cheap petrochemical resources.

Europe is dependent on North Africa for one-quarter of its needs in natural gas. The principal supplier is Algeria. Awareness of the danger of political turmoil in the Maghreb led to the creation in January 1995 of a committee of Southern Europe–North Africa interior ministers whose primary goal is to coordinate measures to cope with terrorism and other forms of political disorder. The ministers meet periodically to share intelligence and to discuss contingency plans to cope with challenges to the established political order in the western Mediterranean region.

This paper addresses three interactive questions, the responses to which could influence the geostrategic equilibrium of the western Mediterranean region in the first years of the twenty-first century.

- Has the EU fashioned a useful topographic map by which to assure effective Maghrebian participation in the EU-Mediterranean partnership program?

- Do the Maghrebian participants have viable alternatives to the Barcelona principles, either in terms of individual initiatives or as part of a subregional grouping?

- What is the capacity of Maghrebian governments to introduce liberal democracy and free enterprise market economy programs consonant with principles outlined in the Barcelona Declaration?

Identification of the principal structural, economic, and political impediments to Maghrebian participation in the widening web of globalization will be undertaken here.

Background of Discussion

Certain underlying assumptions guide this analysis. As the German-French "directorate" of the EU confronts the issues and problems associated with future accession, it will find itself engaged in an exercise in variable geometry.[3] The scope of membership applications is geographically extensive. Of the applicant countries, ten are located in Eastern and Central Europe; two more are in the Mediterranean region; Turkey's membership has been placed in the prenegotiation phase; and the Maghrebian states are in associate status or partial limbo. With the admission of the 13 leading candidates—excluding the majority of Barcelona southern Mediterranean participants—the EU market of 375 million people would increase to more than 500 million, making the union the world's single largest market.

Disagreement already obtains among the majority of EU members concerning admission standards and priorities for accession to be assigned. Disputes have surfaced regarding the lowering of admission standards for the favored few and the likely impact of such lowering on the core membership. The Maghrebian countries are not likely to be beneficiaries of the emerging debate; the Eastern and Central European candidates are themselves engaged in a labor of Sisyphus in efforts to absorb the growing number of regulations (acquis)—in the hundreds—that have poured forth from the European Commission bureaucracy in Brussels.

After the difficult issue of admission standards, a second consideration is building hesitation among EU members concerning the future locus of institutional decision-making authority: the notion of flexibility. This precept, which would accord members freedom to identify regulations and decisions they are prepared to accept or reject, is under discussion in several capitals. Flexibility is recognized by some as a halfway station to devolution, thus expanding the reach of variable geometry. At the other end of the geometric design is France's proposal for creation of a membership core, or pioneering policy group; this has been greeted with reserve by the United Kingdom and others on grounds that the French approach would inevitably lead to formal rank ordering of members.

A consensus is beginning to emerge that favors the creation of a constitution, one setting forth a division of competencies vis-à-vis the EU, nation-states, and regional authorities below them. In substance, the new constitution would seek to satisfy those who desire a clearer statement guaranteeing the future of the nation-state. Southern Mediterranean governments, however, would not be consulted but could be adversely affected by decisions taken, thus further weakening their support for continued participation in the Barcelona process. Debate within EU precincts will be lengthy and arduous, and there is little likelihood that all issues will be resolved by midterm in the coming decade.

The Maghrebian governments have it right in their cautious response to a core element of the 1995 Barcelona Declaration—the adoption of democratic principles and practices for the sharing of domestic political power. The most recent elaboration, setting forth criteria by which standards will be honored (a form of litmus

---

3. Variable geometry refers to a form of EU integration that allows member states to choose whether they wish to participate in any union activity.

test), arose in July 2000 during a U.S.-sponsored international conference on democracy convened in Warsaw, Poland. The Warsaw Declaration, drafted by participants, noted that although democratic governments may vary in a number of particulars, they should meet certain performance standards—treat citizens equally under the law, respect religion and the press, abstain from torture and arbitrary arrest, and guarantee opposition political parties and trade unions the right to organize. Interested Maghrebian parties were afforded an opportunity to observe application of the general standard when Austrian officials were subjected to EU opprobrium when an ultraconservative party, the Freedom Party, was invited to join the country's governing coalition after democratic elections were held in 1999.

In a bullying mood, individual EU members decried the inclusion of the Freedom Party as a violation of EU political and cultural values. In late 2000, EU members had retreated from sanctions vis-à-vis the government of Austria.

To the dismay of Washington, the government of France refused to approve the Warsaw Declaration: France contended that democracy is a complex evolutionary process that gestates and grows within each country and, therefore, sweeping generalizations should be avoided. Situations within accession candidate countries as well as those having associate status should, according to the official French view, be weighed on an individual basis with due consideration accorded historical and cultural factors.[4] Given the 1999 debacle over the Jorg Haider issue in Austria, countries of the Maghreb perceive the possibility that the Barcelona process will yield comparable interventions, ostracism, or sanctions should southern Mediterranean governments fail to meet EU democracy-building standards.

Should relations between Moscow and NATO Europe become strained in the years immediately ahead, or should the Arab-Israeli peace process unravel, threatening widening conflict between Israel and its Arab neighbors, the implications would most likely be serious. An even more likely contingency would be EU failure to fashion strategies and provide the resources to ameliorate economic concerns expressed by governments that border the western Mediterranean basin. Untoward consequences for EU-Maghrebian relations would attend such denouements. Barring such denouements, the Maghrebians—given their existing fraternities of common interest—are not likely to slip existing anchors that tie North Africa to Europe.

---

4. The French position is the correct one because it seeks to avoid rigid standard setting.

CHAPTER 2

The Basic Template of Ties

OVER THE PAST QUARTER CENTURY, the EU and the North Atlantic Treaty Organization (NATO) have convened an array of conferences, seminars, and assorted official gatherings intended to build ties with southern Mediterranean governments. Until 1972, the European Community (EC, forerunner of the EU) conducted relations with Mediterranean nonmember governments on a bilateral basis. The community sought through negotiation and commercial agreements with nonmember governments to establish multilateral ties while it simultaneously accepted the primacy of individual member's political, social and cultural interests. On the other hand, in 1957 the Treaty of Rome made clear the need to establish a common economic external policy while it offered few, if any, guidelines that addressed resolution of outstanding political disagreements.[5]

During much of the 1960s, North Africa's governments, for their part, sought to coordinate negotiation with the EC on a regional basis in an effort to enhance their bargaining position, but the attempt foundered as a result of rising Moroccan-Algerian political tensions and border conflicts.

Before Barcelona

The creation of the Arab Maghreb Union (UAM) in 1989 was welcomed by the European Community as a "pole of cooperation," one that could provide a baseline from which to widen the community's economic role in the Mediterranean basin. Such expectation was reflected in the community's 1990 Revised Mediterranean Policy (RMP), which sought to create a special financial envelope to promote "horizontal cooperation" in the Mediterranean basin.[6] The 1991 Gulf War and the onset of civil war in Algeria derailed effective implementation of the RMP, however.

The 1992 Lisbon Summit, which convened in the midst of the Maastricht Treaty ratification process and the dramatic deterioration of the security situation in Algeria, produced a declaration that explicitly linked the challenges of developing a common foreign policy and adjusting the community approach to the Mediterranean. The declaration, which is of more than passing interest, stated that the Maghreb should receive priority consideration in any future common foreign and security policy (CFSP) that might be hammered out by the EC members and endorsed a Euro-Maghreb framework for cooperation "in every domain." John Calabrese recently noted, "Thus, for the first time, the Community authorized an

---

5. John Calabrese, "Beyond Barcelona: The Politics of the Euro-Mediterranean Partnership," *European Security* 6, no. 4 (Winter 1997): 86–110.

6. Ibid.

approach that was 'global' in substantive, not just nominal, terms."[7] However, the widening crisis in Algeria set back efforts at Maghrebian economic cooperation as outlined under the terms of the 1989 Arab Maghreb Union Treaty. Fearful that the conflict would spread to neighboring Morocco and Tunisia, the EC's successor, the EU, turned toward negotiation of bilateral accords to ensure stability in both countries. The primary vehicles were individual association agreements.[8]

Barcelona Conference

The 1995 Barcelona Conference expanded EU plans for Mediterranean cooperation to include political, cultural, and security matters. The conferences set 2010 as the target date for a regional free trade agreement (FTA) in industrial goods between the EU and its twelve Mediterranean partners and pledged $6 billion in aid for education and infrastructure projects over the initial five years. However, the balance sheet of Euro-Mediterranean partnership (EMP) in providing economic assistance has proved disappointing. Dialogue in the political sector has been problematic. Only a handful of confidence-building measures have been adopted, and talks intended to regulate political and security relations have registered limited progress by the partners, despite lengthy discussion. Here, once again, variable geometry has come into play. The EU is not a state but an economic entity sui generis. France, the primary interlocutor with the Maghreb, is a postmodern state. The Maghrebians retain a premodern patrimonial state structure.

Particularly disappointing for the Maghrebian governments has been the displacement of their region as a "core" or "priority" candidate for EU financial assistance. They are now embedded in a broader Mediterranean constellation and must vie with others for shrinking EU financial resources. Equally troubling, the entire Mediterranean grouping has been accorded diminished standing vis-à-vis Eastern Europe.

Promises

Barcelona promised mutual advantages for the Maghreb and southern Europe. The declaration's rhetoric appeared to augur a new chapter in trans-Mediterranean relationships, predicated on three partnership objectives:

- Strengthen political interaction for the purpose of establishing measures to assure peace and stability in the region;

- Create shared prosperity through formation of free trade zones; and

- Enhance development of human resources intended to promote improved understanding between different cultures, and encourage establishment of civil societies within participant states.

---

7. Ibid.
8. Ibid.

The 15 EU member states and 12 Mediterranean partners attending the Barcelona conclave anticipated the newly minted relationship would provide a foundation for economic, political, and foreign policy cooperation beyond 2010, the target date for creation of a Mediterranean free trade zone. The EU is dominant as the Mediterranean trade partner. An estimated 55 percent of the region's imports and 44 percent of its exports were generated or absorbed by the union in 1998. This was two times the level of the nearest external competition.

The Maghrebian participants also had reason to anticipate that, given their special bilateral ties with France, Spain, and Italy, North Africa would continue as a special beneficiary in the economic realm and special consideration would be accorded to political interests of Maghrebian regimes. Since 1969, the European Community had repeatedly affirmed in official declarations that political stability in Morocco, Algeria, and Tunisia was a quintessential underpinning for continued European prosperity. Although Europe denied formal community membership under the terms of the Treaty of Rome, Europe accorded preferential treatment to the francophone southern Mediterranean states, implicitly providing them informal membership status. Quasi accession was reflected in a variety of preferential trade agreements, financial (loan) arrangements, and expanded investment flows. As a result, North African economies benefited (statistically) with double-digit growth figures until the mid-1990s. Benefits were not evenly distributed, however; Tunisia proved the most advantaged and Algeria the least, despite its strong petro-chemical position. Of more than passing interest is the fact that remittances from North Africans working in Europe dwarfed Community-EU financial assistance to the Maghreb throughout the 1970–1993 period.[9]

Until the midpoint of the 1990s, the Maghreb continued enjoy special recognition in official EU communiqués. In a typical EU acknowledgement, participants in the June 1992 Lisbon European Council confabulation advised that the Maghreb "constitutes the southern border of the [European] Union. Its stability presents a common important interest of the Union." The council proposed that "priority be given to the following actions: promoting a constructive dialogue aimed at creating an area of peace, security, and prosperity in which fundamental principles of international law would be applied…."[10]

Disappointments

The Lisbon communiqué foreshadowed Barcelona 1995. In the wake of the Lisbon meeting, however, the international geostrategic landscape was undergoing transformation. The Warsaw Pact of Soviet satellite states had evaporated in 1989, and by 1991 the Soviet Union itself had imploded, leaving Eastern and Central Europe to draw their own conclusions about Marxist verities. Conservative governments in Western Europe had begun to dissolve on the threshold of the 1990s. Thatcherism and social democrats were on the defensive as unemployment rates rose, economies came under increasing strain, and post–World War II social welfare programs were

9. Lionel Fontagne and Nicolas Peridy, *The EU and the Maghreb* (Paris: Organization for Economic Cooperation and Development [OECD], Development Center, 1997), 3.
10. Ibid.

pressed by intractable demands from aging populations. Shortly thereafter, the collapse of the former Yugoslav federation was attended by brutal ethnic wars that achieved depths of barbarity unknown to Europe since World War II.

Ineluctably, the balance of Western Europe strategic attention shifted eastward to confront demanding agendas, principal among them engagement with Russian leaders dedicated to privatization and introduction of free market economic systems (using shock therapy) and adoption of democratic practices. In southern Europe and the eastern Mediterranean—described as new arcs of strategic crisis—the officially announced European burden was to secure cessation of ethnic conflicts through a combination of traditional diplomacy and, where necessary, military intervention.

For the Maghreb, these shifts in strategic templates had far-reaching consequences. Barcelona represented a shift away from established military, economic, and financial planning vectors, in particular, a veering from Cold War thinking about the meaning of security, with its traditional emphasis on nuclear deterrence, conventional force readiness, and robust power projection capabilities. Doomsday threat perceptions had dissolved, and policy agendas were shifted eastward to enlarge boundaries of political stability and orderly change. The military dimension was relegated to subsidiary importance.

Security assumed new meaning at Barcelona; economic, political, and cultural considerations were bundled together in special status, especially in the western Mediterranean region. A widened panoply of policy problem areas were identified, including internal challenges to governing institutions, transnational migration, human rights abuses, and economic dislocation. The concept of security was transmuted at Barcelona; the panoply of challenges were to be met in a series of properly orchestrated initiatives by the EU and its southern Mediterranean partners. However, to the extent that the EU viewed Islam as a threat to European values, security collaboration would prove impossible because political disorder in the Maghreb would be perceived as having extremist Islamist origins instead of resulting from economic and social dislocations.

The notion of cooperative security quickly gained favor in post-Barcelona European chanceries; the main concern was establishment of mutual confidence by southern Mediterranean participants in EU economic and political initiatives. In the process, history deflected EU attention from the Maghreb. As the Barcelona assembly came to closure, most EU members felt constrained to address unfolding relationships with East Europe, the Balkans, Russia, Ukraine, and the trans-Caucasus. The EU sought to reassure Mediterranean partners that the EU did not intend to abandon the Barcelona concepts but instead was adopting an all-things-to-all-peoples approach.

Nevertheless, frequent reassurance failed to ease Maghrebian disappointment. In official Maghrebian circles, window dressing aside, the belief has grown that the principal EU goal in the Mediterranean is fostering continued Maghrebian economic dependence on Europe while holding at arm's length Arab immigrant populations. Tunisian foreign minister Habib Ben Yahia subscribed to this view following the Barcelona meeting, observing that EU initiatives could only prove effective if the EU persuaded "the young to remain in their countries by mounting projects which create jobs."[11] If the EU countries continue to opt for an immigration containment strategy toward the Maghreb, the two parts of the Mediterranean space will add to Maghrebian mistrust.

Reality in 2000

The EU today envisages a two-pronged strategy. One is intended to encourage trade and financial ties between southern Mediterranean states, thus transforming traditional competitors into regional cooperants. The second approach is to enhance bilateral ties between the North and the South. (Ultimately, the envisaged Mediterranean free trade zone would be facilitated and undergirded by encouraging networks of bilateral ties.) Free trade through bilateralism has, indeed, become the great hope of the EU. However, the OECD observed in a 1997 report that:

> Serious doubt remains…. The free trade agreements with the EU signed in 1995 by Morocco and Tunisia might not generate significant export gains, because these countries' industrial goods already enjoy de facto free access to the EU, and European concessions on food products have been very limited. Conversely, the progressive removal of Moroccan and Tunisian tariffs will not only cause a substantial net loss of tariff revenues but also induce a significant rise in their imports from the EU. That could lead to a highly negative impact on their balance of trade. An estimated 60 percent of industrial firms in Morocco and Tunisia could not survive against freely imported, competing European products unless appropriate technological and marketing improvements are made by 2010.[12]

The OECD report also notes that the EU's planned financial commitments are not sufficient to compensate for the loss of past preferences. It concludes: "The Maghreb countries' stability is at stake. Should macroeconomic imbalances worsen and investment capital be insufficient, government commitments to trade liberalization could slacken and migration pressures could increase."[13] This is precisely what has occurred, thus reawakening European fears that southern Europe is once again on the verge of fresh waves of migrants—legal and illegal.

Given Cyprus's anticipated accession to full EU membership halfway to the 2010 free trade target date and special preferences to be accorded Turkey as it awaits admission, the Maghreb relationship with the EU is not likely to mature into full partnership; nor is any significant new form of economic relationship likely to evolve over the coming decade.

Policy Inconsistencies

Existing EU policies vis-à-vis the Maghreb are characterized by numerous inconsistencies, most notably union efforts directed toward integrating itself more deeply

---

11. Ibid., 8.
12. Ibid., 10.
13. Ibid., 17.

into an increasingly liberal globalized world market while maintaining discriminatory policies toward the Maghreb. The most blatant inconsistencies follow.

- The principle of EU trade preferences for the region is at variance with existing global trade liberalization approaches if North African countries remain excluded from future EU membership. More fundamentally, preferential policies adopted by the EU have narrowed opportunities for industrial expansion in the Maghreb while they have simultaneously inhibited North African exports of food products.

- EU trade policies for the Maghreb countries have been discriminatory, engendering qualitatively different impacts on Moroccan and Tunisian agricultural exports to Europe.

- The avowed promotion and diversification of the Maghreb's exports, two main objectives of the EU's trade and financial policies, are at odds in the absence of effective financial support for emerging sectors of specialization.

- The consistency of migration and financial policies is also questionable. Given political constraints on labor flows, capital mobility becomes crucial. Promoting capital mobility requires credible signals to the market through new financial instruments and the use of privatization as a means of signaling an intended increase in EU financial obligations (which are not presently available).

- Compensation for the transitional costs of Maghreb trade liberalization through an FTA raises another issue. As the region's economies open their domestic markets to foreign competitors and EU firms take on important market shares, a concession from the EU should consist of extensive financing facilities. Yet the notion of offsetting compensation has certain disadvantages: liberalization would enhance the competitiveness of Maghreb industries over the long term. However, near-term adjustments in areas such as worker dislocation and private investment would be socially painful. The question then becomes not one of compensating trade liberalization but one of addressing which measures should be adopted to ease the pain of heavy external payments difficulties associated with a rise in Maghreb imports as liberalization stimulates the Maghreb countries faster than their structure changes to yield greater export competitiveness.[14]

Economic Incompatibilities

A number of economists question the incompatibilities of EU external policies. Some economists perceive a conceptual gap between EU protestations of interest in integration of Mediterranean countries in a liberalized world market while it maintains discriminatory policies and practices, for example, implementing an industrial export policy for southern Mediterranean partners while excluding agricultural products, determining inconsistent bilateral assistance levels, and

14. Richard A. Falk and Tamás Szentes, eds., *A New Europe in the Changing Global System* (New York: United Nations University Press, 1997), 183.

providing special benefits for certain financial institutions. Eberhard Kienle and others have argued that partnership may well have more negative than positive consequences for states along the southern rim of the Mediterranean. Recommended policies of internal and external economic liberalization, in their view, could well have an adverse impact on prospects for economic growth in terms of job creation, investment, productivity, and expanded technological capability.[15]

The experiences of the former Soviet republics, now the Commonwealth of Independent States (CIS), with economic liberalization strategies and the adoption of EU guidelines are hardly reassuring for the Maghreb. Shock therapies advised by Brussels, the United States, and the World Bank have proved painful for the majority of Eastern and Central European governments, as reflected in rising unemployment, depressed world market conditions, EU proprietary approaches to structural and legal reform, and adverse consequences experienced during the financial crisis in Russia (1998–1999). It is noteworthy that output performance by a number of CIS countries—most of which had remained major trading partners with Russia—during 1998 and 1999 deteriorated such that aggregate GDP fell by more than 0.5 percent from the previous year's level, a "considerable slide from the 2 percent growth achieved in 1997," according to a report by the United Nations Economic Commission for Europe.[16]

Note also that economic decline has served to undermine traditional Marxist social policies intended to maintain satisfactory levels of employment, maintain high fertility rates, and provide (in theory at least) adequate social welfare nets. With adoption of capitalist policies, declines have occurred in the share of benefits—such as maternity and child allowances—to families with children and in family income. In several instances, generous child-raising leave has been reduced or completely eliminated. Taken together with falling real wages, the impact on family integrity and social fabric has been deleterious. These trendlines in Eastern and Central Europe have not escaped the attention of governments in the Maghreb, where profound reservations exist concerning the risks and consequences likely to flow from adoption of the full panoply of EU partnership guidelines.

Despite the uneven performance of the Eastern and Central European aspirants for EU accession, the union commission continues to insist that southern Mediterranean partners replicate major aspects of the European single market within their own countries. The commission has in mind established norms for income growth, reduction of external debt, privatization of state enterprises, and harmonization of customs procedures with those obtaining in EU Europe. Only by moving vigorously to meet these standards can the southern Mediterranean states expect to be in position to become competitive at the international level and gain further access to European markets.

Harmonization, however, ignores the fact that Maghrebian economies lack resources to meet the growing needs for production facilities, electronics, transport vehicles, food storage, and manufacture of heavy-duty farm equipment. Governments in the Maghreb are compelled to look to Europe and others to meet these

15. *Annual Report* (Paris: OECD, 1999), 234.
16. Ibid.

domestic requirements. Resurrection of the five-nation Arab Maghreb Union, embracing Morocco, Algeria, Tunisia, Libya, and Mauritania, that was established in 1989 to create a regional industrial and trade base, is a distant dream. (Even if rehabilitated, the Maghreb's infrastructure foundations are fragile at best.) The UAM has failed to surmount internal divisions and has registered few break-throughs in efforts at regional economic cooperation; its members continue to rely on bilateral ties with Paris, Madrid, and Rome to sustain hopes for economic growth and development.

Political Stability in the Maghreb

The Maghrebian governments quite evidently are ill prepared to shoulder the likely social costs and political uncertainties that would almost certainly arise should they embrace EU proposed strategies. If the Eastern European experience is a meaningful portent, losses in job creation and productivity would have to be overcome. In the domestic political arena, attendant dislocations—ineluctably perceived as having been imposed by Europe—would undermine what popular support exists for the governing institutions and the legitimacy of the state.

Before tectonic changes in government policies can be contemplated, extensive dialogue with interest groups within each Maghrebian state would be requisite. Representative public and labor organizations, regional and tribal influentials, small entrepreneurs, and civic associations would require reassurance. All are heavily dependent on the patrimonial governing system that currently obtains in much of North Africa. A number of scholars have observed that governments in the Maghreb confront daunting challenges in managing changes in regime-state-nation relationships. Any alteration is perceived as threatening a breakdown in international order. Regimes, therefore, cling to the status quo.

Globalization strategies propounded by Europeans have other systemic implications for Maghrebian governments. For member states, globalization in EU terms suggests the erosion of national boundaries, the spread of modern technologies that unleashes the flow of information to politically active populations, and the rise of transnational intrusive actors such as the OECD, the UN, sundry humanitarian associations, and nongovernmental organizations. Europeans, while occasionally chafed by intrusive interventions on the part of such actors, see them as "soft" security issues and do not believe them to represent serious challenges to regime legitimacy. For North African governments, however, European "soft" security matters are primordial, tightly interwoven, and therefore share pride of place with "hard" security.

The Tunisian government appears most receptive to the EU paradigm for globalized development, but it, like Algeria and Morocco, is wary of the potentially destabilizing impact to the existing political order. The government of Algeria views the Internet as a medium that has the capacity to undermine state institutions by fueling public skepticism concerning the efficaciousness of adopted policy. In the cultural realm, globalization has the potential to undermine a fragile sense of national identity that is yet to be fully embedded in society as well as corrode traditional Islamic and communal values. Where international issues dominate, the internal dynamics of domestic society tend to be perceived by ruling parties as having a dominant role in influencing the stability of the state. The protection of national sovereignty at this point is believed by governments in the Maghreb to be of greater importance than the political, economic, and cultural paradigms currently being offered up for emulation by the EU, the United States and others. Although some seasoned observers suggest that the Maghrebian societies might succeed in borrowing the best of Western economic reform models without sacrificing traditional values—as Japan and Thailand have done during the past three decades—the prospect for a substantially more than incremental approach is problematic, at least during the first decade of the twenty-first century.

The issue of stability also suffers from disjunctures in perspective. EU members tend to think that privatization and democratic power sharing, good governance, and the encouraged growth of representative political parties are promising approaches by which to assure political stability. The EU will concede, albeit implicitly, that it must wink at political disfigurement under authoritarian regimes as in Algeria and Libya to assure member states undisturbed access to petrochemical resources at cheap prices. Lenience for Algeria can be justified since Algeria appears to be emerging from a near-decade-long nightmare of civil war. Hence, it is mutually advantageous to accept that the government of Algeria will not deign to view "soft" political process issues in terms comparable with those dear to the heart of the Europeans. Democracy and human rights safeguards, Algeria contends, cannot overshadow government efforts to control divisive centrifugal forces that threaten fledgling national institutions.

Particularly vexing to Maghrebian governments have been the unmet promises of economic aid proffered by the EU after Barcelona. The economic basket was the most detailed component of the Barcelona Declaration. It was designed to achieve economic development in a region in which demographic increase outpaced economic growth. In constant-dollar terms, subsidies to Maghrebian states since 1995 have not matched EU rhetoric and are today woefully incommensurate with Maghrebian needs.

The World Bank, on the other hand, has compiled a commendable record and has plans to buttress economic investment programs and restructuring efforts by Morocco, Algeria, and Tunisia. Loans exceeding $1 billion are pledged to strengthen Moroccan productivity in the communications sector; reorganize and diversify Algeria's banking system, especially the operations technology sector; and broaden the base of Tunisia's economic industrial development. World Bank efforts in the Mediterranean basin are also directed toward widening and liberalizing intra-Arab trade in the Maghreb region, where speculation has grown about creation of a common market.

Feeble Partnership Foundations

Globalization threatens to place severe constraints upon the autonomy of states. Robert Cox has brilliantly analyzed the potential costs of participation in the emerging international regime:

Globalization is generating a more complex multi-level world political system, which implicitly challenges the old Westphalian assumption that a state is a state. Structures of authority comprise not one but at least three levels: the macro-regional level, the old state (or Westphalian) level, and the micro-regional level. All three levels are constrained by a regional economy which has means of exerting its pressures without relying on formal authoritative political structures.[17]

The pressures of globalization are thrice magnified in North Africa, where structures of authority at most levels are feeble at best. As a result, globalization from the Maghrebian perspective necessitates dependence on the laborious EU bureaucratic processes and on the good will and intentions of former colonial masters. For some Maghreb officials, the partnership does not reflect the substance of these relationships. An interaction among equals is patently absent. Instead, the relationship is reflective of a satellite status on the part of Mediterranean partners.

Other, more open-minded officials have adopted somewhat more hopeful views. They acknowledge that the trajectory of economic ties with Europe is heavily dependent on sustained economic growth within the EU community. The OECD has presented a relatively optimistic outlook for EU Europe. It estimates for the year 2000 a 3.5 percent or better economic growth rate for France, Germany, Spain, and the Netherlands, accompanied by modest reductions in unemployment levels. Job creation in Spain, France, and Germany has grown—in part because of part-time and temporary hire strategies adopted by their governments and business communities. (Spain's unemployment rate, however, remains mired at 15 percent—centered largely in urban areas. Farm communities in southern Spain remain dependant on Moroccan workers' seasonal labor, much as does the United States vis-à-vis Mexican farm workers.) The OECD, while taking note of improved EU member states' gains in economic performance, observes that these gains are not equally distributed among the membership and cautions that current economic upticks should not be viewed as a portent of future long-term (5–10 year) growth rates.[18]

Beset by economic woes, Maghrebians are rankled by the appearance of discrimination. For example, the admittance to European Union membership in 1996 of Spain and Portugal had adverse economic consequences for Morocco and Tunisia, then major exporters of agricultural products. The price reference system—which had provided special countervailing tariffs to ensure that North African and European pricing structures would be equivalent—was abandoned. In the aftermath of Lisbon-Madrid accession, the EU substituted a quota system pegged to the average export levels of Moroccan agricultural products during the period 1980–1984—a time of severe drought in North Africa and, hence, depressed agricultural output.[19]

---

17. Robert Cox, "Structural Issues of Global Governance: Implications for Europe," in *A New Europe in the Changing Global System*, eds. Falk and Szentes, 59.

18. *Economist*, June 10, 2000, 53–54.

19. Until 1992, the EC proved singularly resistant to any proposal for basic alterations in the relationship even though it appeared to discriminate. In January 1992, however, the European Parliament rejected the EC commission's Fourth Financial Protocol proposal for Morocco and Syria on the grounds of their human rights abuses. Morocco riposted by rejecting the principle of the aid protocols and canceling a fishing agreement with the EC, which severely damaged Spanish and Portuguese fishing prospects because fleets from both countries depend on access to Moroccan and Western Saharan waters. In May 1992, the EC patched up the quarrel by offering Morocco a free trade agreement, which is eventually to be extended to the whole of North Africa except Libya, and providing a 46 percent increase in fishing fees under a new EC-Morocco fishing agreement. *Economist* Intelligence Unit, *Country Report: Morocco* no. 2 (1992): Business International, 8–9.

CHAPTER 3

The Travails of Morocco

S PAIN AND PORTUGAL HAVE BEEN ABLE TO SEIZE an economic advantage owing to their admission to EU membership; Morocco and Tunisia have seen only limited benefits from their associate status. Spain's gross domestic product (GDP) per person is today 12 times that of Morocco's. These widening disparities will be impossible to overcome during the coming decade.

Accommodation to the EU

The government at Rabat remains under pressure to accommodate EU interests. For example, it felt required during 1999 to accede to the terms of a new Association Agreement with the EU to replace the 1976 European Community Accord. Hailed by EU commission representatives at the signing ceremony as a manifestation of "widening and deepening" of second-generation Barcelona strategies intended to foster "new fields of cooperation such as political dialogue and cultural exchange," the agreement was officially presented as complementary to economic partnership. However, some Moroccan specialists interviewed in Rabat during June–July 2000 viewed the new Association Agreement as European pressure to undertake not only extensive EU-recommended economic reforms but also far-reaching changes in social programs (e.g., improved national education standards and women's rights) to achieve what is viewed in Brussels as the necessary transformation of what is essentially an archaic (feudal) system.[20]

Economic Policies

Particularly disturbing to Moroccans attending the unveiling of the new association accord was acknowledgement by EU commission participants that delay in achieving final approval had occurred as a result of union procedure that required 15 member states ratify the agreement before completion of the negotiating processes. The lengthy delay in ratification—four years to completion—was attributed to Spain's need for unfettered access to Moroccan fishing grounds. During 1995, Madrid and Rabat were found to be at loggerheads over renewal of an existing fisheries agreement involving extension of rights in Morocco's 200-mile exclusive fishing zone. In theory, two outstanding issues—Moroccan agriculture and EU access to fishing grounds—were to be treated as separate and distinct issues. But Spain claimed the support of the 14 other EU members in rejecting the Moroccan

---

20. One of several interviews conducted by William H. Lewis, June–July 2000. At the request of the interviewees, assurances are honored concerning nontransparency of sources.

proposal. The situation of stasis worked to Spain's advantage. The two issues became inextricably linked during the negotiations despite EU denials to the contrary. In due course, a single state—Morocco—of the Southern Mediterranean 12 was compelled to surrender major fishing concessions to EU solidarity. The patent disadvantages to Morocco of EU multilateral solidarity have not been lost on the Moroccan government.[21]

The new Association Agreement includes a five-year (2000–2006) National Indicative Component (NIP) for Morocco, reflecting the following EU priorities:

> First, support for…economic reforms, particularly in the form of sectoral adjustment programmes. Second, MEDA [Mediterranean Economic Development Activity] will concentrate on the development of the private sector through direct support to Moroccan companies. Third, MEDA II will accompany the Moroccan government's efforts for a better social balance and the fight against poverty. The Social Development Agency, for example, will carry out actions for those people most vulnerable; actions will also be carried out to foster the integration of Moroccan women. Furthermore, the programme for Morocco's developed northern provinces will be continued. Finally, MEDA II will develop additional means in order to strengthen the civil society, for the promotion of human rights and the environment.[22]

Social Issues

The EU policy dedicated to enhancement of the status of Moroccan women had startling consequences. Several weeks after announcement of the policy, the Moroccan monarch, Muhammad VI, announced plans to introduce precedent-setting social and political reforms, only to find his proposal greeted with massive public demonstrations.

EU concern about the benighted northern Moroccan provinces, long ignored by the young ruler's autocratic father, Hassan II who died in 1999, was attributed to illicit migration of Moroccan youths to Spain, which is separated by a mere 8 miles from northern Morocco. The two Spanish presidios (places of sovereignty) of Ceuta and Melilla located in northern Morocco had become focal points for passage of undocumented workers and export of narcotics (kef) to Spain. Moroccan kef exports earn Morocco a reported $2 billion annually. Also, West Africans in growing numbers use Moroccan ports for illegal migration as well as for money laundering. The EU has proposed that EU immigration officers be permitted to police Moroccan ports—a request received in Rabat as an affront to Moroccan sovereignty.

The EU has taken official notice of the difficulties posed by Morocco's northerners by funding construction of a 10-foot-high perimeter fence at Melilla. The EU's deputy head of the Maghreb unit and desk officer for Morocco observed on March 1, 2000 that the problems "range from drug exports and youth unemployment to illiteracy and the sluggish development of rural northern areas." But in a

---

21. John Damis, "Morocco's 1995 Fisheries Agreement with the European Union: A Crisis Resolved," *Mediterranean Politics*, issue 3.2 (September 1999).

22. *EUROMED* (special feature) no. 13, March 7, 2000, 2.

startling assessment of the state of all Morocco's rural areas, the official observed: "Within 30 years, they will reach a Western level of prosperity."[23]

The foundations for this pessimistic assessment are not difficult to discern. Recurring drought cycles have weakened agricultural output; lean taxes and low foreign investment have strained revenue availability; inadequate educational infrastructure has also had a drag on technical competence in both the government and the commercial sectors. Agriculture, a mainstay of the Moroccan economy as an employer of labor and the national granary, has remained static at best even in non-drought years. The sector is deficient in modern farm equipment, financial subsidization, and seasonal agricultural storage facilities. With uncertainties attending drought cycles, widespread rural unemployment has forced increased numbers of unemployed workers (*chomeurs,* who are 25–30 percent of the labor force) into Moroccan cities, where crowded living conditions and constricted employment opportunities serve as combustible social and political elements. Morocco's economic plight—during a 10-year period (1988–1998) of government liberalization with undistinguished results—has engendered the existing undocumented labor migration to Europe, including the worrisome brain drain of technically trained Moroccan youths.

Jean-Pierre Turquoi, in a special article published by *Le Monde* in March 2000, offered a grim assessment:

> Quelques chiffres donnent la measure des problèmes de fond de royaume. Comme le faisait observer récemment un groupe d'économistes marocains, entre 1991 et 1999, le nombre de pauvres a fait un "fantastique bond en avant", passant de 3,5 à 5,3 millions d'individus alors qu'il avait fortement baissé les années précédents. Aujourd'hui, les 10% de Marocains les plus riches consomment quatorze fois plus que les 10% les plus pauvres. Plus de la moitié de la population est analphabète et un enfant sur deux en âge d'être scolarisé ne fréquente pas lécole. La mortalité maternelle est la plus élevée du monde arabe. Dans les campagnes, moins de un ménage sur cinq a accès à l'eau potable. Pour l'électricité, le ratio est à peine plus élevé.
>
> Le chômage est un autre révélateur des difficulteés économiques. En 1982, il atteignait 10% de la population active. Il est acutellement de 16%, et bien davantage (de l'ordre de 25%) en milieu urbain. Principale population affectée: les femmes et les jeunes, qui'ils soient diplômés ou non.[24]

Individual Assessments

A series of informal interviews in Europe and the Maghreb during June–July 2000 with a wide range of academic experts, EU officials, and government representatives provide useful insight into the parlous condition of the EU-Maghrebian dialogue:[25]

---

23. Ibid., 1.
24. Jean-Pierre Turquoi, "Moroccan Economic Malaise," *Le Monde,* March 23, 2000, p. 5.

Midlevel EU official in Brussels:

We are embalmed in disagreement over our future purposes and goals. North Africa will continue to be viewed as a tertiary issue, one that should be addressed on a bilateral basis by France, Spain, and Italy.

Belgian official:

Globalization implies continued technological and economic backwardness for the Maghreb. The essence of partnership is a continued dependency relationship with Europe. The Maghreb's basic strength is its prevailing weaknesses— illegal immigrants in ever-growing numbers.

Belgian restaurateur:

The Moroccans come to us as an ill-documented underclass. They are willing to work for reduced wages, but they are also burdening our welfare programs. Social unease is growing among my Belgian workers, who believe the EU must address these difficulties.

Moroccans displayed a comparable unease:

Rabat University faculty member:

The EU has marginalized Morocco in its long-term planning, while placing political and economic burdens on Moroccan society. We are expected to open up the economy, to destroy certain economic sectors, to free the media of governmental control, and to radically alter traditional values—all without a promised full membership in the union. This is unacceptable.

Labor union representative:

We do not share common perspectives on the problems and tensions arising among people in our society. They are disappointed and bitter about their prospects in a country in decline. The EU is locked into a certain reform ideology that offers only frustration and dissatisfaction with both the union and our ruling elite.

Moroccan official:

The death of Hassan II was a traumatic experience for many of our people. We are today in processes of transition and new political alignments, each with its own challenges and fresh concerns. We require time to adjust—at a time of widening divisions in society and mounting impatience in some quarters. The EU strategies are not helpful.

---

25. Interviews conducted by William H. Lewis, June–July 2000. At the request of the interviewees, a sampling of representative views is provided while assurances are honored concerning nontransparency of sources.

Tradition under Attack

Moroccan receptivity to EU-recommended economic and social reform initiatives is predicated on untested Brussels assurances that far reaching benefits will ultimately follow for Morocco. EU commissioners, however, refuse to provide safety nets to lighten risks of sociopolitical upheavals that might erupt in Morocco. Moroccan officials observe that EU recommendations, if fully embraced, almost assuredly would require that the regime adopt repressive political measures—a retrograde "achievement" in light of the 1995 Barcelona Declaration. Morocco, politically, is urged by the EU to set aside the autocratic practices of the past and replace them with "good governance" under the watchful guidance of a youthful, inexperienced monarch—unreconnoitered social and political terrain for a country experiencing wrenching economic difficulties.

The chasm between EU rhetoric and perceived dangers is apparent to many Moroccans. For example, the Moroccan government is urged by Brussels to support the revival of the Arab Maghreb Union (UAM), this while EU officials acknowledge that a UAM embedded in a broader southern Mediterranean free trade zone would continue to have marginal bargaining power. Second, the two-track multilateral–bilateral negotiating strategy adopted by the EU actually enfeebles if not actually undermines the union's attachment to Mediterranean subgroupings for purposes of trade negotiations. Third, Morocco's claims for special EU recognition and entitlements are warranted given Spain's claims to sovereignty over Ceuta and Melilla, which raise doubts about whether Spain is partly Maghrebian or purely European.

Some observers believe that Morocco is the litmus test that will determine success or failure for EU initiatives in North Africa. The government of Muhammad VI confronts existential issues. Hassan II, who had ascended the throne in 1961, ruled as a spiritual autocrat and secular despot. The religious leader of the traditional Islamic community, Hassan tolerated little opposition to his mandate—from sources religious or profane contending his feudal authority was by divine right. His successor, Muhammad VI, was not groomed for the role of religious leader, nor did he command appreciable experience as arbiter of competing ethnic, tribal, and religio-political forces. Acclaimed as a promising reformer upon his ascension in 1999, Muhammad became subject to pressures from countervailing domestic forces—all seeking promises of political alignment or safeguards for their inherited power positions and political allies. Some reforms, contemplated under EU inspiration, threatened to undermine long-standing political influence; and rumored social reforms threatened to undermine treasured religious and social values.

In the monarch's publicly perceived ambition to march Morocco from the feudal to the modern, Muhammad was seen to have experienced a traumatizing setback early in 2000. Muhammad VI had asked in one of his first televised speeches: "How can we imagine building a civilized and prosperous community when the interest of women, who represent half of it, are betrayed?"[26] Muhammad's draft legislation proposed to allocate one-third of the 600-plus seats in the national parliament to women (they currently claim four), accord them special protections

---

26. *Economist*, March 18, 2000, 44.

in divorce proceedings, and provide women increased opportunity for education at a time when literacy rates for Morocco's female population are the lowest in North Africa.

On March 12, the government and Islamists staged competing public rallies in the face of the palace's announced plan. In Rabat, the national capital, a hastily organized rally of 40,000 citizens expressed support of the plan. In Casablanca, the national center of modern commerce and trade, 500,000 Islamists and their supporters emerged to denounce the reforms and urge continued adherence to shari'a religious precepts, strait-jacketing women's rights. The massive negative response emanated from unemployed, alienated Casablanca youths and the supporters of the outlawed Islamist movement *Al-Adil wa al-Ihsane* (Justice and Charity), whose leader King Hassan had once consigned to an insane asylum.

Figure 3.1 GDP Per Person, 1999

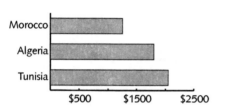

Source: *Economist,* March 4, 2000, 48.

Rebuffed by this negative outpouring, the palace has lost some of its initial ardor for social and political reform, acknowledging that it might be less disruptive for palace influence to assume the mantle of autocrat rather than that of democrat. The security services are once again assuming broadened responsibilities, press censorship has returned, and the palace has recently turned aside IMF-recommended economic initiatives. Many observers believe the economy appears calcified (see the figures on this page), at the mercy of inept, corrupt bureaucrats and a middle class unwilling to forgo palace patronage. Morocco ranks last in economic performance compared with Algeria and Tunisia.

Figure 3.2. GDP Change, 1998–1999

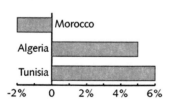

Source: *Economist,* March 4, 2000, 48.

Fewer than 50 percent of Moroccans can read and write; at least 4 million Moroccans live on less than $1 a day; most rural areas are bereft of natal care facilities; more Moroccan mothers die in childbirth than elsewhere in the Arab world; in urban centers, one in four Moroccans is unemployed—a staggering figure that is likely to rise over the coming decade.[27] In the face of these depressing data, most Moroccans are skeptical that the West, or the EU in particular, has a full appreciation of Morocco's economic malaise. For King Muhammad and his coterie of advisers, stability and security are the order of the day. At the political level, despite EU urgings, there is little inclination to participate in processes of liberal democratization—seen as a leap into the unknown that could mortgage the future of the monarchy to forces outside control of the palace.

27. *Economist,* March 4, 2000, 48.

CHAPTER 4

The Way Elsewhere—Algeria

ALGERIA, THE SCENE OF MURDEROUS CIVIL CONFLICT that since 1992 has claimed more than 100,000 lives, is a source of acute discomfort to the EU. Union representatives have visited Algeria from time to time urging political reconciliation only to be rebuffed and to recoil at the human costs of ongoing violence and attendant resulting abrogation of human rights. Senior EU officials have fashioned few effective initiatives to influence the level of violence; neither have they deigned to make Algeria the target of official opprobrium or sanctions. Economic considerations (e.g., energy resource dependence) have been the primordial determinants of EU policy since the outbreak of civil warfare in 1992.

Recent Political Reconciliation

Since mid-1999, however, there has been reason to hope for change. Algeria's tragic civil war appeared to have entered a new, more promising phase when President Liamine Zeroual, a retired military officer, stepped aside as president and national elections were conducted to select a successor. Several political "parties" presented reasonably well-known candidates. Among the first to emerge was Abdelaziz Bouteflika, erstwhile foreign minister for Houari Boumedienne during the 1960–1970 period. Long rusticated in the shadows of retirement, Bouteflika had no apparent party affiliation but was understood to have the tacit support of Algeria's military and intelligence services (*le pouvoir*) long involved in directing a draconian campaign against Islamic extremists and their insurgent allies—the Armed Islamic Group (AIG) and the Islamic Salvation Army (AIS), the latter the guerilla offspring of the Islamic party, the Islamic Salvation Front (FIS), that had been outlawed in 1991–1992. Bouteflika's beginnings were far from auspicious. All rival candidates for the presidential post with the exception of Bouteflika withdrew on the threshold of the national vote, accusing the military of blatant intervention and fraud. Bouteflika, in the wake of his electoral "victory," required eight months to secure *le pouvoir* endorsement of his nominees for cabinet posts.

Bouteflika has registered some notable political successes in a campaign calling for national reconciliation and the return of Algeria to civil normality. The president rapidly unveiled a precise, well-defined action program to achieve these objectives. The first initiative in the plan involved a national referendum, conducted in September 1999, to seek public affirmation for an offer of amnesty to insurgents untainted by "excesses of brutality." The insurgents would be required to present themselves to a probation commission charged with responsibility for investigating past activities of amnesty applicants, an impossible mandate given the murderous nature of the civil conflict. Popular support for the Bouteflika initiative was diluted as tens of thousands of Algerians, themselves victims of AIS and AIG depredation, demonstrated by forming victims' associations to urge public accounting of humanitarian excesses supported by appropriate retribution. The security services intervened to forestall further public demonstrations.

By midyear 2000, the reconciliation strategy had proved partially successful. The FIS leadership embraced the amnesty—despite Bouteflika's refusal to return the party to legal status—and its AIS guerilla force disarmed. Relative calm has been restored to urban centers and a semblance of normality infused into their immediate environs. The situation in rural areas remains unstable, however. The AIG continues to conduct raids against unprotected civilians in western Algeria, and Hassan Hattab's Group for Preaching and Combat (GSPC) provokes an atmosphere of instability in the Kabylie mountain region in the East. Concomitantly, 200,000 armed village militia continue to conduct vendettas and retaliatory campaigns. Victimhood remains ubiquitous in rural Algeria.

Bouteflika has also demonstrated a propensity for theaterlike successes on the international stage. He has attended an array of conferences and meetings, serving as host of the year 2000 Organization of African Unity (OAU) summit in Algiers. He has been a successful intermediary in the Congo crisis, chairman of multiple diplomatic initiatives to end the Eritrean-Ethiopian war, and a proponent of efforts to harmonize diplomatic relations with post-Hassan Morocco in an effort to resurrect the hitherto moribund AMU. In 2000, Bouteflika has received kudos from abroad for these efforts and was lionized during a summer 2000 state visit to France, an apparent anomaly given Bouteflika's anti-Gallic posture in his earlier service as Algeria's foreign minister.

Systemic Problems

A residue of disappointment with Bouteflika's strategies and policies has arisen on the domestic side, however.[28]

■ Sense of Continuing Malaise

> This is an armed country where the gun, the knife, and vengeance continue to rule. Until all elements and *le pouvoir* are called to account, normality will be beyond our grasp. I am not hopeful.   —University scholar

> External influence is readily apparent to a significant number of informed Algerian citizenry. The Pinochet factor is at play, as are the South African experience with post-apartheid reconciliation and the war crimes indictments against leaders in Serbia and Croatia. Criminal prosecution is a specter that *le pouvoir* must take under serious consideration if political and economic change is to occur in Algeria.

---

28. The following quotations are taken from interviews conducted by William H. Lewis, June–July 2000. At the request of the interviewees, a sampling of representative views is provided while assurances are honored concerning nontransparency of sources.

■ Nature of Political Reform

Bouteflika plays off adversaries and colleagues with panache, except for the military. He knows our weak points and where we are susceptible to blandishments. We remain skeptical and unbelieving. Our economic system is like a sleepwalker, afraid to awaken. Our youths are cynical and without promising futures. We remain three societies: one in charge but without a widespread following; the second divided between secularism and the West and those who see ultimate solutions in Islam; the third, rural Algerians with their own divisions and animosities. Syndicalism is caught in an inescapable limbo.

—Labor union organizer

This is not necessarily a representative view but it points to wounds and uncertainties yet to be fully addressed by Algeria's president.

Nor is this to gainsay the progress that has been registered since mid-1999. Some significant reforms are contemplated. Members of parliament, restive with military oversight, have begun to urge adoption of measures to broaden its mandate; calls are also surfacing, however tentative, urging the lifting of the existing state of emergency that severely inhibits political activity. Some even have overcome temerity to propose renewed legal status for the FIS. (The military, however, maintains a studied reserve on these matters.)

More promising has been the unleashing of the press, which has exhibited a certain freedom of spirit and inquiry. Victims' associations have materialized (as previously noted), organizing protests against amnesty for the insurgents without accountability for their depredations and demanding information concerning the fate of thousands of family members who have disappeared—many at the hands of the security services—since the onset of the civil war. Critics of Bouteflika are becoming increasingly impatient over his failure to reform the judiciary (characterized by some as passive drones), the continued high level of unemployment (in excess of 30 percent), and the blatantly low quality of educational instruction (in particular, in modern technology, economics, and executive management).

■ Dilemma of Globalization

We hear of the economic miracles associated with globalization and the march of technology, yet Algeria has no design to catch up. We are a society divided and demoralized, waiting for the end of violence, which may never come. As a result, whole generations of young people are left without resources, training, or hope.   —Graduate student

Algeria today is paying a heavy price for inept leadership, a failure to fulfill social and economic commitments by the ruling elite after Algeria severed its colonial moorings in 1962:

At Evian, France, in 1962, Algerians gained a state before they could claim a national identity. Their only tie with the nation's pre-colonial past was Islam; their only relationship with the state's post-independence leadership…was war and violence. Memories of heroism and delusions of socialism—Arab and otherwise—helped sustain a national idea for the 1960's and early 1970's. As these memories faded, a new generation of younger Algerians who had never known colonization rebelled against formerly heroic leaders whose corrupt and repressive one-party regime were blamed for Algeria's inability to meet raised economic expectations after the dramatic (and unexpected) rise in oil revenues in 1973.[29]

Legacy of Violence

The present crisis did not arise solely out of failed economic planning, maldistribution of government resources, or abortive efforts to introduce democratic political processes in 1989–1990, as many Western observers contend. The current civil war in Algeria has its origins in the immediate aftermath of Algeria's seven-year struggle to liberate itself from French colonial rule. Disagreements over power distribution erupted between political chieftains and local warlords (*wilayists*) who had borne the brunt of the struggle. Disagreements also emerged between ideologues wishing to have emerging state institutions embrace Marxist doctrine and those urging more liberal approaches to governing. Armed conflict erupted among several such competing factions in mid-1962, characterized as the "summer of shame" by many Algerians anxious to get on with postwar reconstruction. With the successful intervention of a newly formed national army, the country was held together through a jerry-built coalition of military commanders; an embryonic civil bureaucracy; and an encrusted, increasingly corrupt political formation, the National Liberation Front (FLN).

For the next quarter century, Algeria remained a work in progress. Its political system was seclusive, its ideological orientation fervently revolutionary, and its governing institutions increasingly incapable of fashioning programs to overcome burgeoning economic and social ills. These failures alienated a youthful population forgetful of the human costs of the liberation struggle, beset by unemployment, and faced with squalid living conditions in Algeria's overpopulated cities. Not unexpectedly, urban rioting erupted in 1988; at least 400 deaths were reported at the hands of the police. The Algerian governing triad, scandalized and in disarray, collapsed in 1988–1989.[30]

The remaining leadership under President Chadli Ben Djedid attempted to fashion a new, viable political system that included national and local elections with participation by secular and religious parties. As the 1980s came to closure, the FIS, a coalition of diverse religious and secular elements, emerged as a leading contender for the reins of power. Its platform consisted of an array of solutions to the national crisis that were predicated on religious principles and vaguely formulated remedial action programs. Although many Algerians voted for FIS candidates during national and local elections in protest against continuing triad leadership, few were prepared to endorse the more doctrinaire precepts espoused by extremist clerics.

---

29. Simon Serfaty, "Algeria Unhinged: What Next? Who Cares?" *Survival* 38, no. 4 (Winter 1996–1997): 147.

30. William H. Lewis, "Algeria at 35: The Politics of Violence," *The Washington Quarterly* 19, no. 3 (Summer 1996): 3–18.

Being a coalition of the alienated instead of a well-structured political party, FIS cohesion could be sustained only through continued victories in the electoral processes then under way.

Role of the Military

The usurpation of the electoral process by the Algerian military, dedicated to pursuit of secular goals and security missions, led to widening conflict, a conflict attended by unbridled savagery and rising casualties within the civilian population. The government headed by President Liamine Zeroual attributed the atrocities to Islamic extremists, notably the out-of-control AIS, an offshoot of the banned FIS.[31] Although no independent source validated claims of more than 100,000 deaths resulting from the civil war, doubts began to arise about the capacity and willingness of the military-backed government to safeguard its citizens. Increasing calls from outside Algeria for an inquiry to establish the veracity of government claims led the EU to dispatch a delegation to Algiers during the 1998 Ramadan season with a mandate to initiate discussions about the security situation. Its investigation was ill-received and proved unproductive.

The military directorate shaping policies and strategies in 2000, officially known as the *Haut Conseil de Sécurité,* has persisted in its contention that protection must be accorded the institutions of the state. National order remains the highest priority and, as corollary, coercive instruments are to be directed against those dissident factions and groups that seek to undermine the legitimacy of state institutions. The military directorate, in pursuit of this "sacred" mission, has adopted a multitiered strategy to "control evolutionary changes":

- Continuation of the counterterror campaign in an effort to eradicate militant Islamist groups;

- Introduction of programs of far-reaching economic reform to bolster the economy and restore public confidence in government performance; and

- Participation by compliant political parties and religious groups in the shaping and management of government plans and strategies for liberalization of the national economy.

A no-exit military strategy is in place, one intended to perpetuate security-service oversight as the guardian of Algeria's transition to a second republic. There is no intention to do so, however, despite occasional Western exhortations that the military return to the barracks. The directorate believes that Islamist extremism and the AIG represent a clear and present danger given their demand that the vocabulary of Islam replace that of Arab secular nationalism.[32] The directorate is not a spent force, and it believes it remains capable of producing viable national institutions and a political system that overcomes the nation's numerous economic and social ills.[33]

---

31. In mid-2000 the AIS accepted cease-fire and amnesty, however.
32. The AIG did not accept cease-fire and amnesty.

An Outlook of Reform

The Bouteflika administration, for its part, declaims his government is dedicated to overcome "immobility" on reform programs. He is emphasizing political reform and liberalization of economic policies, privatization, and encouragement of foreign investment. Witness Bouteflika's dismissal of a reluctant prime minister in October. In addition, the government is seeking legislation to strengthen banking and investment laws, acknowledging that the public sector can no longer assume all burdens for wealth creation. It is presently seeking to overcome bureaucratic resistance to his public policy priorities.

Other vested interests are addressed as well, notably labor organizations concerned with protection of worker rights, family groups seeking to open employment opportunities for youths, regional interest groups, and small-scale entrepreneurs hesitant to deal with the exigencies of open-market competition. Algerian officials have noted in interviews that all these groups are ill-disposed to accept shock therapies required for liberalization and privatization.[34] The private sector is populated largely by small family enterprises whose survival has depended on government largess and petty corruption. To achieve an open, modern economy, public willingness to accept painful alterations in traditional practices is necessary if Algeria's nonenergy sector is to be organically linked with the technologically advanced economies of Europe.

Government officials acknowledge that full linkage will not occur until Algerian society is no longer in conflict with itself. At present, a civil society is not fully emergent. The political environment must first undergo fundamental transformation; there must also be unrestricted access to information, awareness of the country's economic infirmities must be noted by political parties, and reform strategies debated; and labor must fashion approaches that attack national problems constructively. Problem-solving time constraints are mounting. Approximately 450,000 youths are entering the employment ranks each year but Algeria can absorb fewer than 100,000, with the remainder certain to become marginalized and alienated. They will seek exodus from Algeria in growing numbers, with Europe as their final destination. An estimated 2 million Algerians already reside in France. The pressures of migration—legal and illegal—are leading some French politicians to observe: "France is suffering neocolonialism in reverse, 'a la Algerie.'" In Europe, the EU stands as the frontier between affluence or decline. Across the Mediterranean, the EU is perceived as an imperial wall that must be brought down to ensure economic opportunity.

Barcelona 1995 heralded a strategy of trans-Mediterranean partnership that was to have two strategic axes. The first was to be multilateral in dimension with three points of reference—first, economic cooperation and free circulation of goods leading to a Euro-Mediterranean free trade zone; second, political dialogue on a multilateral basis with particular emphasis on peaceful resolution of disputes

33. William H. Lewis, *North Africa: Crisis Management at the Margins*, Occasional Reports in European Studies (Washington, D.C.: CSIS, June 1998), 30.

34. Interviews conducted by William H. Lewis, June–July 2000.

and mutual security; third, respect for democratic principles and fundamental human rights. In the instance of Algeria, the security objective (domestic internal order and political stability) and the adoption of liberal democratic principles (shared political power outside military constraint) are in inherent tension. The EU relationship remains defined by economic considerations, with France viewed by most union members as responsible for the heavy lifting on political and economic issues vis-à-vis Algeria. The EU's economic contribution has been directed toward completion of an Algerian gas pipeline that has proved of economic benefit to Spain and Portugal.[35]

France's ties with Algeria are both profound and intimate. The brutal seven-year war for independence lacerated Moslems and, by 1962, led to the flight of 1 million French settlers to their mother country. Yet, almost four decades after independence, French cultural influence among Algerian intellectuals and the majority of the urbanized populace is firmly entrenched. French television programs are readily available and enthusiastically received; Algerian-born soccer stars are enlisted to serve on France's front-rank teams and are frequently honored in both France and Algeria; French politics and intellectual thought are closely followed and influence the perceptions of the emergent Algerian middle class. An Algerian physician recently observed:

> I am deeply indebted to France for my professional training and cultural orientation. My family and I vacation in the Loire whenever possible and we have subscriptions with three of France's best journals. However, when I return to Algiers from vacation I feel depressed by the absence of France when called upon to support our democratic aspirations. We have been abandoned by Paris for reasons I fail to comprehend.[36]

The physician has ample justification for complaint. Official France has lent firm support to the succession of military-controlled governments that perpetuate emergency powers, initially for fear that national elections might catapult Islamic extremists to power and, more recently, because of fears that violence unchecked would destabilize Morocco and Tunisia—a denouement that might engender uncontrolled refugee flight to southern Europe.

William B. Quandt, who has evaluated Algeria's efforts to secure an exit from authoritarianism, states:

> While Algerians have never poured into the streets demanding democracy, there is nonetheless evidence that they want the chance to choose their own government. They complain about the *hogra* of their rulers, their arrogance and aloofness, and the contempt they show for ordinary citizens. This is not the attitude of a passive or complacent electorate. When given the chance to vote, large

---

35. The pipeline extends for 1,370 kilometers between Hassi R'Mel (Algeria) and Cordoba (Spain), including a 525 km section in Morocco and 45 km under the Strait of Gibraltar. In the official view of the EU, the pipeline "constitutes the most spectacular of the economic binding of North Africa to the European Union." The gas pipeline will transport annually 6 billion cubic meters of natural gas to Spain and 2.5 billion to Portugal. Morocco will receive 1 billion cubic meters.

36. Interviews conducted by William H. Lewis, June–July 2000.

numbers of Algerians have actually gone to the polls…. Algerians do not demand democracy, but they seem eager to have the chance to rid themselves of rulers they do not like. And that, after all, is one of the core principles of democracy.[37]

Professor Quandt acknowledges, however, that ongoing violence—particularly revenge-taking in the crucible of unmanageable conflict—is a problem seemingly beyond government resolution. The prevailing atmosphere stifles efforts to anchor civil society in rule-of-law practices. The *pouvoir* remains suspicious of forces seeking a democratic opening. Algeria during much of the 1990s became the Middle Eastern state with the greatest incidence of domestic violence, a dubious distinction at best. A firmly established civil society, representing all the diverse sectors of Algeria, appears a distant hope. Existing trade associations and civil interest groups remain anemic, faction riven, and without the capacity to shape public attitudes on national and regional agendas. As Quandt wrote, Algeria remains a nation without a societal and political center of gravity, a work in progress that will take decades to complete.[38]

---

37. William B. Quandt, *Between Ballots and Bullets: Algeria's Transition from Authoritarianism* (Washington, D.C.: Brookings Institution, 1998), 157.
    38. Ibid.

CHAPTER 5

Tunisia—Opportunities Found, Opportunities Misplaced

T HE TUNISIAN GOVERNMENT PERCEIVES ITSELF as well-positioned to serve as the jewel of the Middle East and North Africa. It is fortunately placed by geography, history, and dint of effective planning to serve as successor to Beirut as it was during its glory days. The casual visitor to Tunisia is struck by its sense of centrality, both geographically in its relationship with the EU and with Europe more broadly. Geography, however, also bears a negative imprint. Clamped between conflict-ridden Algeria to the west and Qadhafi-ruled Libya on its eastern border, Tunisia is at the mercy of problematic forces over which it can exercise little influence.

Continuing Authoritarianism

President Zine El Abidine Ben Ali, a former army officer and national security chief, assumed the presidency in 1987 after rusticating aging "president for life" Habib Bourguiba and offering Tunisians hope for relaxation of the latter's stringent security measures. These hopes—founded on release of political opponents from incarceration, expanded press freedoms, and assurances of new political rights for fledgling parties—evaporated when the government adopted authoritarian measures. Western observers attributed the new draconian approach to official protestations of alarm over the substantial showing by Islamist activists—an estimated 12 percent nationally and 30 percent in several major urban centers—during national elections held in 1989. In their wake, President Ben Ali's security services announced that Islamist extremists had been discovered to be engaged in coup plotting; hundreds were arrested, the Islamist party outlawed, and its leader forced into international exile. Tunisian political and press freedoms have since been increasingly circumscribed.

Some indication of the nature and extent of authoritarian measures in effect was noted by Jean-Pierre Turquoi in an article published by *Le Monde* on the threshold of a presidential election held in October 1999:

> On 24 October the Tunisians are to elect a president for a period of five years. And, for the first time, they will have the choice between three candidates: outgoing President Zine El Abidine Ben Ali, and the leaders of two marginal political parties. Celebrated to saturation point in the national press, this "progress" does not really amount to much. The outgoing president...has suc-

31

ceeded in skillfully selecting his false adversaries by means of an amendment to the constitution. Rather than casting a shadow over Ben Ali, they will serve to show him off to very best effect in an election that holds no suspense. Winning 90 percent of the votes at the previous elections, everyone is agreed that his score will be almost as high on this occasion.

The columnist then proceeded to observe:

Why would it be any different? Tunisia is not by any stretch of the imagination a democracy. Islamists are hunted down and exiled, while secular opponents are imprisoned. The Judicial system is ready to do as it is told. The police exercise tight control throughout the land.[39]

In retribution, several follow-on issues of *Le Monde* were banned from circulation in Tunisia.

Economic Advancement

Public quiescence toward such security constraints has been attributed by most European observers to economic and social advances registered since the 1987 palace coup. Government initiatives have transformed Tunisia from a "near basket case" into one of a meager number of economic success stories in the Arab world. Its improved economic performance has won plaudits from the World Bank, the EU, and from the French government. The EU signaled its appreciation by concluding a free trade partnership agreement in 1995 that was the envy of other Mediterranean regimes.

There is much merit in Tunisia's economic performance over the course of the 1990s. The number of Tunisians considered below the poverty level has declined from 30 percent to 6 percent. Women's rights have made the country a leader in the Arab world. Education and literacy rates have evinced remarkable improvement. Indeed, as Jean-Pierre Turquoi remarked in his October 1999 article:

[L]iving conditions for Tunisians are improving all the time, and they know they have their president to thank for it. There are virtually no slums left in Tunis and homes have water and electricity. Life expectancy has risen five years over the past decade. There is a doctor for every 1,500 inhabitants. Schooling for children, and especially for girls, reaches levels others can only dream of. Tourism is expanding [in excess of 4 million visitors per annum]. The administration is modernizing. To be a homeowner and drive a car is no longer a luxury but the norm for most of the middle classes who can receive low-interest loans.[40]

Not surprising, as a result, have been tangible expressions of approval by the World Bank—a major lender—and the EU. The EU has shown appreciation in the form of a Euro-Tunisia enterprise business center in Tunis (costing 20 million

---

39. Jean-Pierre Turquoi, "Tunisia Continues Its Modernization," *Le Monde*, October 5, 1999.
40. Ibid.

ecu[41]); a credit of 30 million ecu by the European Investment Bank for private companies undergoing modernization; and, inter alia, support (40 million ecu) for Tunisian government programs intended to upgrade occupational training to meet challenges posed by the worldwide revolution in technology.[42]

Despite these material gains, the Tunisian government has reacted hesitantly to EU proposals urging basic adjustments in the private investment and financial sectors. Lisa Anderson has dissected the Tunisian strategy:

> As should be apparent by now, the regimes of North Africa have for decades adroitly played what political scientists call "two-level games" by employing domestic policy for foreign purposes—providing "labor peace" for potential investors and undertaking economic reform to obtain conditional loans—and using foreign polity for domestic purposes—claiming their hands are tied by the International Monetary Fund or by the demands of national security....
> [T]hey have continued to carefully monitor the international scene, hoping to replace the international leverage their strategic position had provided during the Cold War with some new claim on Western attention. The idea that the litmus test for American aid would no longer be anticommunism but, say, actual observance of human rights was for obvious reasons genuinely worrisome.[43]

Clearly, Tunis has achieved favored status on the part of the International Monetary Fund and the World Bank. However, the fund, in its 1999 annual performance assessment, was critical of the pervasive role of the government, observing that Tunis must "speed up the liberalization of prices and the rate of privatization of public companies in order to boost economic efficiency and favor job creation."[44]

Hopes for EU Attention

The Ben Ali government has based its political–economic strategy on the expectation of strengthened relationships with the EU. The president hopes to demonstrate in the process that economic growth and overall prosperity are essential requisites for political stability, preconditions for the introduction of multiparty participatory democracy. To compress the timetable for far reaching political reform could have untoward consequences in the view of the government. For the moment, the government believes, political change should only occur at the margins; and, in this interim, Paris should be placing Tunis more fully into the EU economic slipstream. These views have received weighty considerations in French and EU Commission policy circles, but there is little likelihood that Tunisia will be placed at the head of the EU-southern Mediterranean class.

The Ben Ali government has reason to anticipate EU preferential treatment. Tunisia was the first southern Mediterranean country to have signed an association

---

41. European currency unit.

42. *Euro-Mediterranean Partnership* (Brussels: European Commission, 1997), 25.

43. Lisa Anderson, "Prospects for Liberalism in North Africa," in *Islam, Democracy, and the State in North Africa*, ed., John P. Entelis (Bloomington: Indiana University Press, 1997), 137.

44. Turquoi, "Tunisia Continues Its Modernization."

agreement with the union (July 17, 1995), an agreement that covers a wide range of fields including education, culture, economic cooperation, and scientific research. Social and political dialogues are a central part of Tunisia's partnership process, at least theoretically. It is, however, in the fields of trade, investment, and industrial development that Tunisia places its highest expectations.

During the 1992–1996 ninth economic plan, Tunisian economic performance deserved applause: an average annual GDP growth rate of 4.6 percent, reflecting high productivity in the manufacturing and service sectors; an increase in exports at an annual rate of 6.3 percent in constant prices; an annual average inflation rate below 4.8 percent; and balanced use of public expenditures for the purpose of limiting the national budget deficit to an average of 3.5 percent of GDP. The government has also registered major progress in the social area, reflecting efforts to improve living conditions in various parts of the country, particularly remote regions; for example, the rate of rural electricity supply increased from 29.3 percent in 1984 to 63.7 percent in 1994; the rate of access to safe water stood at 68.3 percent in 1994; and has risen substantially since; family homes and general apartment housing now meets 70 percent of national requirements. Some imbalances have materialized, however. For example, agriculture as a share of GDP decreased to less than 13 percent in 1998–1999.

The government has recently introduced its ninth plan, an ambitious undertaking intended, in the words of official communiqués, to achieve the "total integration of the nation in the international economy." The ninth plan, as announced, is intended to:

■ Establish a free trade area with the EU, in part by strengthening the performance and output of Tunisia's private sector;

■ Increase the pace of job creation and commodity exports;

■ Develop and modernize the nation's infrastructure;

■ Upgrade human resources to afford Tunisians opportunities to take full advantage of the technology information revolution; and

■ Encourage regional economic development to ensure that economic benefits are shared as equitably as possible.

The ninth plan is exceedingly ambitious in terms of its stated goals and targets. For example, the Ben Ali government proposes to increase the country's annual economic growth rate to 6 percent per year, in part by focusing on increased productivity in new areas such as communications, finance, and services in general. In addition, the government will seek to ensure a growth rate of 6 percent (at constant prices) for exports of goods and services, excluding the energy sector. The objective of this plan is to reduce the country's adverse trade balance.

Despite a reasonable economic performance, Tunisia has not overcome a number of difficulties. It must cope with an extremely fragile banking system. Also, the government has anchored its political control to Tunisia's emergent middle class, making use of heightened consumption and readily available credit as a means for securing middle class loyalty. There are very few consumer credit companies and, in the absence of legislative guidelines, retail outlets and others tend to grant credits over an extended period at exorbitant interest rates. At present, widening indebtedness increasingly funds overconsumption. Defaults on bank loans have further weakened a poorly positioned banking system: the level of nonperforming loans—loans never likely to be repaid to the banks—is above 20 percent and the level of nonrecoverable debts exceeds $2 billion, double Tunisia's revenue from privatization over the past decade.

Today Tunisia reposes in the category of an emergent economy. The country's success or failure in efforts to become a full participant in the processes of globalization depends heavily on benefits that France and the EU are prepared to bestow on it. Although there have been discussions in Brussels concerning the liberalization of intra-Arab trade, approximately three-quarters of Tunisian trade remains rooted in Europe. Following this, some Arab governments have reduced their customs tariffs with Arab neighbors by 10 percent. Informed observers advocate the intensification of efforts by the Arab Maghreb countries to liberalize trade and integrate their economies. Also, there has been a discussion about establishing a Maghreb common market, partly to offset the EU's competitive advantage vis-à-vis the southern Mediterranean Arab states. However, local rivalries and political disputes have impeded effective progress on intra-Maghreb economic cooperation.

In the aftermath of the 1993 Israel-Palestine Oslo agreement, which set Palestinians on the path to independence, the U.S. government briefly sought to establish a multilateral economic framework that would encourage Arab trade and other forms of economic collaboration with Israel. Unfortunately, the fall 2000 outbreak of *intifada* violence and stern countermeasures by Israel undermined the U.S. strategy.

Hence, Tunisia currently has no readily available exit from continuing to depend on the EU for its economic lifeline. At the onset of the new century, however, the EU is also dependent on Tunisia as an Arab-world lodestar for the Barcelona partnership. To ensure the viability of their partnership with Tunisia, France and other European Union members appear increasingly prepared to sacrifice the Barcelona principles of conditionality and transparency on the altar of pragmatism and political stability.

CHAPTER 6

Horizons Near and Far

THE SENSE OF URGENCY THAT SEIZED EU THINKING about the Maghreb early in the 1990s has eased substantially. The transition in Morocco from the 30-year rule of King Hassan to that of his youthful son, Muhammad, has been negotiated without dramatic strain, and some effort is being made to reinvigorate the national economy. President Bouteflika of Algeria, despite some flamboyant excesses, has succeeded in reducing the level of violence that once threatened to carry Algeria to the abyss of national breakdown and, most notably, has secured the disbandment of the largest insurgent group, the AIS. Tunisia, under President Ben Ali, exhibits all the benefits of middle-class economic expansion while it denies political empowerment to the less advantaged majority. Overall, early 1990s European fears of a radical Islamist tidal wave have abated, and trade ties with Arab participants in the Barcelona partnership show signs of modest growth.

Most EU members have little time and few national interests to pursue in their relations with Maghrebian states. Since the mid-1990s, an atmosphere of benign neglect has evolved. Officials in Brussels continue to schedule conferences, symposia, and workshops with Mediterranean partners and compile impressive official communiqués and opaque public pronouncements. For their part, southern Mediterranean participants, particularly the Maghrebians, have grudgingly accepted a constricted role in setting conference agendas, populating the secretariats, and fashioning the language of official declarations. Roberto Albioni has recently underscored this point:

> The institutional machinery of the EMP (Euro-Mediterranean Partnership) does not fully reflect the notion of partnership, that is, equal participation in a venture. This is essentially for two reasons: first, the Senior Officials Committee is chaired by the revolving EU presidency instead of revolving among all partners, that is among non-EU partners; second, the work of the two institutional EMP Committees, the Euro-Med Committee and the Senior Officials' Committee is prepared and followed up by the services of the European Commission and the EU Council instead of by its own secretariat....[45]

Albioni has urged that this imbalance be rectified by according EMP committees greater independence from the EU and commission structures, thereby diminishing the excessive influence of the commission bureaucracy in shaping and implementing decisions taken in the guise of EMP action programs.[46]

---

45. Roberto Albioni, "Resetting the Euro-Mediterranean Security Agenda," *The International Spectator* 33, no. 4 (October–December 1998): 5.

46. Ibid.

Several other discernible points of divergence need to be addressed by the Barcelona partners. Key among them are measures to be adopted by European regional and various other international organizations in planning and integrating economic and financial subventions to each of the Maghrebian recipients. At present, despite best intentions, the EU and its several agencies have failed to coordinate plans and programs with the IMF and the World Bank—as well as with the United States and other contributing countries. An apparent lack of consensus exists on such matters as debt relief; programs in education; redress of denial of women's rights; and codes to be adopted to enhance foreign investment, trade, banking. A frequent complaint heard recently in the region has concerned the confusing and frequently contradictory advice proffered by various foreign organizations. Assistance provided by these organizations is dependent on recipient acquiescence, but crosscutting, rival proposals appear to have impeded effective performance by the confused hosts of well-intentioned foreign advisers.

A further fault line relates to EU ambivalence concerning obligations the union itself should assume when it urges the Maghrebians to adopt its formulas for economic reform. The countries that would endure the 5–10 year period of social dislocation and attendant economic privation that would accompany these reforms would require substantial foreign assistance to alleviate the resultant stresses of transition. EU safety net programs are not in sight and, according to commission representatives in Brussels, little relief is contemplated in light of the heavy decision-making burdens confronting the union over widened membership and constitution-making.[47]

Inescapable, however, is the need to fashion mutually agreed strategies to deal with the widening irritations arising from the dark underside of existing European-Maghrebian social-economic difficulties—the mounting tide of illegal immigration by North Africans, production and shipment of home-grown narcotics, black marketeering, and comparable illegal enterprises that have a negative impact on Western Europe. For many West Europeans, the main threat to their cultural identity comes from immigrants and asylum seekers from the Arab world who create their own society and cultural environment within the national society they enter. Restrictive legislation contemplated by European governments, while seemingly justified, is perceived by Maghrebians as discriminatory and confirmation that the Euro-Maghrebian partnership is intrinsically inequitably balanced in favor of EU interests.

Given Maghrebian dependence on access to Europe's market, however unbalanced the terms of access, bruised feelings are not likely to engender total estrangement. Realistic Maghrebian assessment of the tone and texture of relations will almost certainly continue to be influenced by domestic economical political imperatives of Maghrebian regimes and their heavy dependence on trade ties with Western Europe. The Maghrebians must deal with forces that, for the moment, appear beyond their control—globalization, shifting international financial markets, and revolutionary changes in telecommunications and information technology. These needs arise at a moment when the center of decision-making

---

47. William H. Lewis, interviews conducted in Brussels, June–July 2000.

gravity is shifting away from the old guard in Morocco, when Algeria's security services must calculate gains and losses in continuing to maintain harsh measures against perceived threats to state institutions, and when Tunisia's Ben Ali must devise fresh plans to sustain his country's previous economic performance. Failure to meet those challenges would confront Europe with its worst nightmare—a region of widening political and social instability that deeply discomforts and worries the European mainland.

CHAPTER 7

The United States—
A Partner or a Marginal Actor?

DOES THE UNITED STATES HAVE A CONSTRUCTIVE ROLE TO PLAY or is the United States likely to continue to concentrate its diplomatic energies and economic resources in the eastern Mediterranean region and the Persian Gulf? At the height of the Cold War, North Africa was an area of substantial strategic importance to Washington. Morocco made facilities for intelligence collection available to the U.S. Navy, which could then monitor movements of the Soviet Mediterranean squadron. Morocco also provided political–military resources for crisis management in sub-Saharan Africa. In addition, King Hassan proved a valuable moderating influence in episodic Arab-Israeli crises. As testament to Hassan's value, the United States lent diplomatic and military backing to the monarch during 1975–1985 after he seized control of the Western Sahara—formerly a Spanish colony—to quell insurgency on the part of the Polisario. The Polisario, supported by Algeria, Libya, and the Soviet Union, were a constant threat to Moroccan control of the Western Sahara.

Similarly, Washington established close diplomatic and security ties with the Tunisian government in the wake of a 1981 Qadhafi-inspired filibustering expedition that threatened to topple the regime of the pro-Western president, Habib Bourguiba. From Washington's perspective, Rabat and Tunis (together with Cairo) served as promising counterpoises to pro-Soviet governments in Libya and Algeria.[48]

While North Africa's strategic importance has diminished substantially with the demise of the Cold War, Algeria has continued to remain a source of official concern to the U.S. government. At initial glance, the United States would appear to have only a marginal interest in Algeria's ongoing trauma. The Clinton administration, in 1993–1994, tended to look to France on policy issues relating to Algeria (much as it looked to the United Nations and the EU to cope with the 1992–1995 crisis in Bosnia). The few policy pronouncements on Algeria that emanated from Washington called for the peaceful settlement of the civil conflict and were generally ill-received in Paris and Algiers. Following the presidential election held in Algeria in 1995, however, President Clinton wrote to his Algerian counterpart pledging support as long as President Zeroual continued his efforts at reconciliation with various domestic groups, including the FIS leadership. The U.S. government predicated its support for Zeroual on signs of continuing progress in

---

48. Despite widespread popular opposition, the governments of Tunisia and Morocco provided diplomatic support to Washington during the 1991 Gulf War.

the direction of broader democracy and the adoption of liberal economic reforms. In early 1998, disturbed over the growing violence in Algeria, the United States altered its official posture and called for an international inquiry to identify and condemn parties involved in the massacre of the civilian population. The military directorate strongly objected and, to this date, continues to resist third-party efforts to investigate the parties held responsible for attacks on the civilian population and other human rights violations.

During civil wars, security forces almost invariably are suspected of complicity in violating human rights and of turning a blind eye to atrocities by local militias. In the case of Algeria, ample ground existed for such suspicion. The levels of savagery experienced in early 1998 were not unexpected; intelligence relating to AIG plans were readily available; ample opportunity existed for the security services to organize rapid response forces to deal with the outbreaks of violence. The military itself had organized hundreds of militia forces that were theoretically linked to its command-and-control system. Press reports in 1998 and 1999 clearly indicated that some militia forces were embarked on campaigns of vengeance taking against the AIG and its civilian supporters. Should this violence persist, the Bouteflika government will be subject to EU pressure to clean up its act—as one Union official declared in mid-2000.[49]

To the extent that Algeria emerges as the major regional actor over the next several years, U.S. policy in the North African region will have to be reformulated. The new administration in 2001 cannot evade the need to reassess the existing abstemious U.S. posture, which largely defers to the EU on western Mediterranean issues. Simon Serfaty recently observed:

> Now, even as memories of the Cold War fade, every EU decision has a U.S. dimension, and every U.S. decision can have an EU dimension. That such would be the case is one of the most lasting legacies of the Cold War, not because it means the resurrection of the United States as a European power but because it confirms its status as a power in Europe…. [I]t is an informal non-member state of the EU. Thus, the indispensability of the U.S. engagement is hardly a matter of false sentimentality. Rather, it is a question of genuine interests that are not matched, in toto, in any other region of the world outside the Western Hemisphere….[50]

For the new U.S. administration to defer to the EU to resolve North–South issues would present Brussels with insupportable burdens, which might well derail European efforts at creation of a wider and deeper European community. Beginning in 2001, Washington will be required to assess its commitments to Western Europe and its driving force, the EU. Trade disputes will undoubtedly arise and blur common economic imperatives and national security interests. Early in 2001, however, joint consultation in search of common goals in North Africa should be initiated with a view to delivering effective strategies that address the multitude of

49. William H. Lewis, interview conducted in Brussels, June–July 2000.

50. Simon Serfaty, *Europe 2007: From Nation-States to Member States* (Washington, D.C.: CSIS, January 2000), 17.

issues and challenges confronting diverse governments in the southern Mediterranean regions.[51]

---

51. In the wake of the Barcelona conference, from which the U.S. government was excluded at French behest, the U.S. Department of State initiated a general review of U.S. policy in the Mediterranean basin. The review, initiated by Under Secretary of State Thomas Pickering, brought together several bureaus with special concerns in the region. Its purpose was to fashion a post-Barcelona strategy directed toward greater overall coherence in policy. The review failed, in large measure owing to the competing interests and goals expressed by each of the participating department bureaus. Secretary of State Madeleine K. Albright resisted efforts to organize or follow a strategy in review.

Barcelona Declaration Adopted at the Euro-Mediterranean Conference

Barcelona, 28 November 1995

Final Version 2 Rev. 1

(27 and 28 November 1995)

- The Council of the European Union, represented by its President, Mr Javier SOLANA, Minister for Foreign Affairs of Spain,

- The European Commission, represented by Mr Manuel MARIN, Vice-President,

- Germany, represented by Mr Klaus KINKEL, Vice-Chancellor and Minister for Foreign Affairs,

- Algeria, represented by Mr Mohamed Salah DEMBRI, Minister for Foreign Affairs,

- Austria, represented by Mrs Benita FERRERO-WALDNER, State Secretary, Ministry of Foreign Affairs,

- Belgium, represented by Mr Erik DERYCKE, Minister for Foreign Affairs,

- Cyprus, represented by Mr Alecos MICHAELIDES, Minister for Foreign Affairs,

- Denmark, represented by Mr Ole Loensmann POULSEN, State Secretary, Ministry of Foreign Affairs,

- Egypt, represented by Mr Amr MOUSSA, Minister for Foreign Affairs,

- Spain, represented by Mr Carlos WESTENDORP, State Secretary for Relations with the European Community,

- Finland, represented by Mrs Tarja HALONEN, Minister for Foreign Affairs,

- France, represented by Mr Hervé de CHARETTE, Minister for Foreign Affairs,

- Greece, represented by Mr Károlos PAPOULIAS, Minister for Foreign Affairs,

- Ireland, represented by Mr Dick SPRING, Deputy Prime Minister and Minister for Foreign Affairs,

- Israel, represented by Mr Ehud BARAK, Minister for Foreign Affairs,

- Italy, represented by Mrs Susanna AGNELLI, Minister for Foreign Affairs,

- Jordan, represented by Mr Abdel-Karim KABARITI, Minister for Foreign Affairs,

- Lebanon, represented by Mr Fares BOUEZ, Minister for Foreign Affairs,

- Luxembourg, represented by Mr Jacques F. POOS, Deputy Prime Minister and Minister for Foreign Affairs, Foreign Trade and Cooperation,

- Malta, represented by Prof. Guido DE MARCO, Deputy Prime Minister and Minister for Foreign Affairs,

- Morocco, represented by Mr Abdellatif FILALI, Prime Minister and Minister for Foreign Affairs,

- the Netherlands, represented by Mr Hans van MIERLO, Deputy Prime Minister and Minister for Foreign Affairs,

- Portugal, represented by Mr Jaime GAMA, Minister for Foreign Affairs,

- the United Kingdom, represented by Mr Malcolm RIFKIND QC MP, Secretary of State for Foreign and Commonwealth Affairs,

- Syria, represented by Mr Farouk AL-SHARAA, Minister for Foreign Affairs,

- Sweden, represented by Mrs Lena HJELM-WALLEN, Minister for Foreign Affairs,

- Tunisia, represented by Mr Habib Ben YAHIA, Minister for Foreign Affairs,

- Turkey, represented by Mr Deniz BAYKAL, Deputy Prime Minister and Minister for Foreign Affairs,

- the Palestinian Authority, represented by Mr Yassir ARAFAT, President of the Palestinian Authority, taking part in the Euro-Mediterranean Conference in Barcelona:

- stressing the strategic importance of the Mediterranean and moved by the will to give their future relations a new dimension, based on comprehensive cooperation and solidarity, in keeping with the privileged nature of the links forged by neighbourhood and history;

- aware that the new political, economic and social issues on both sides of the Mediterranean constitute common challenges calling for a coordinated overall response;

- resolved to establish to that end a multilateral and lasting framework of relations based on a spirit of partnership, with due regard for the characteristics, values and distinguishing features peculiar to each of the participants;

- regarding this multilateral framework as the counterpart to a strengthening of bilateral relations which it is important to safeguard, while laying stress on their specific nature;

- stressing that this Euro-Mediterranean initiative is not intended to replace the other activities and initiatives undertaken in the interests of the peace, stability and development of the region, but that it will contribute to their success. The participants support the realization of a just, comprehensive and lasting peace settlement in the Middle East based on the relevant United Nations Security Council resolutions and principles mentioned in the letter of invitation to the Madrid Middle East Peace Conference, including the principle land for peace, with all that this implies;

- convinced that the general objective of turning the Mediterranean basin into an area of dialogue, exchange and cooperation guaranteeing peace, stability and prosperity requires a strengthening of democracy and respect for human rights, sustainable and balanced economic and social development, measures to combat poverty and promotion of greater understanding between cultures, which are all essential aspects of partnership,

- hereby agree to establish a comprehensive partnership among the participants the Euro-Mediterranean partnership through strengthened political dialogue on a regular basis, the development of economic and financial cooperation and greater emphasis on the social, cultural and human dimension, these being the three aspects of the Euro-Mediterranean partnership.

Political and Security Partnership: Establishing a Common Area of Peace and Stability

The participants express their conviction that the peace, stability and security of the Mediterranean region are a common asset which they pledge to promote and strengthen by all means at their disposal. To this end they agree to conduct a strengthened political dialogue at regular intervals, based on observance of essential principles of international law, and reaffirm a number of common objectives in matters of internal and external stability.

In this spirit they undertake in the following declaration of principles to:

act in accordance with the United Nations Charter and the Universal Declaration of Human Rights, as well as other obligations under international law, in particular those arising out of regional and international instruments to which they are party;

develop the rule of law and democracy in their political systems, while recognizing in this framework the right of each of them to choose and freely develop its own political, socio-cultural, economic and judicial system;

respect human rights and fundamental freedoms and guarantee the effective legitimate exercise of such rights and freedoms, including freedom of expression, freedom of association for peaceful purposes and freedom of thought, conscience and religion, both individually and together with other members of the same group, without any discrimination on grounds of race, nationality, language, religion or sex;

give favourable consideration, through dialogue between the parties, to exchanges of information on matters relating to human rights, fundamental freedoms, racism and xenophobia;

respect and ensure respect for diversity and pluralism in their societies, promote tolerance between different groups in society and combat manifestations of intolerance, racism and xenophobia. The participants stress the importance of proper education in the matter of human rights and fundamental freedoms;

respect their sovereign equality and all rights inherent in their sovereignty, and fulfil in good faith the obligations they have assumed under international law;

respect the equal rights of peoples and their right to self-determination, acting at all times in conformity with the purposes and principles of the Charter of the United Nations and with the relevant norms of international law, including those relating to territorial integrity of States, as reflected in agreements between relevant parties;

refrain, in accordance with the rules of international law, from any direct or indirect intervention in the internal affairs of another partner;

respect the territorial integrity and unity of each of the other partners;

settle their disputes by peaceful means, call upon all participants to renounce recourse to the threat or use of force against the territorial integrity of another participant, including the acquisition of territory by force, and reaffirm the right to fully exercise sovereignty by legitimate means in accordance with the UN Charter and international law;

strengthen their cooperation in preventing and combating terrorism, in particular by ratifying and applying the international instruments they have signed, by acceding to such instruments and by taking any other appropriate measure;

fight together against the expansion and diversification of organized crime and combat the drugs problem in all its aspects;

promote regional security by acting, inter alia, in favour of nuclear, chemical and biological non-proliferation through adherence to and compliance with a combination of international and regional non-proliferation regimes, and arms control and disarmament agreements such as NPT, CWC, BWC, CTBT and/or regional arrangements such as weapons free zones including their verification regimes, as well as by fulfilling in good faith their commitments under arms control, disarmament and non-proliferation conventions.

The parties shall pursue a mutually and effectively verifiable Middle East Zone free of weapons of mass destruction, nuclear, chemical and biological, and their delivery systems.

Furthermore the parties will consider practical steps to prevent the proliferation of nuclear, chemical and biological weapons as well as excessive accumulation of conventional arms.

Refrain from developing military capacity beyond their legitimate defence requirements, at the same time reaffirming their resolve to achieve the same degree of security and mutual confidence with the lowest possible levels of troops and weaponry and adherence to CCW.

Promote conditions likely to develop good-neighbourly relations among themselves and support processes aimed at stability, security, prosperity and regional and subregional cooperation.

Consider any confidence and security-building measures that could be taken between the parties with a view to the creation of an "area of peace and stability in the Mediterranean", including the long term possibility of establishing a Euro-Mediterranean pact to that end.

Economic and Financial Partnership: Creating an Area of Shared Prosperity

The participants emphasize the importance they attach to sustainable and balanced economic and social development with a view to achieving their objective of creating an area of shared prosperity.

The partners acknowledge the difficulties that the question of debt can create for the economic development of the countries of the Mediterranean region. They agree, in view of the importance of their relations, to continue the dialogue in order to achieve progress in the competent fora.

Noting that the partners have to take up common challenges, albeit to varying degrees, the participants set themselves the following long-term objectives:

■ acceleration of the pace of sustainable socio-economic development;

■ improvement of the living conditions of their populations, increase in the employment level and reduction in the development gap in the Euro-Mediterranean region;

■ encouragement of regional cooperation and integration.

With a view to achieving these objectives, the participants agree to establish an economic and financial partnership which, taking into account the different degrees of development, will be based on:

■ the progressive establishment of a free-trade area;

■ the implementation of appropriate economic cooperation and concerted action in the relevant areas;

■ a substantial increase in the European Union's financial assistance to its partners.

A) FREE-TRADE AREA

The free-trade area will be established through the new Euro-Mediterranean Agreements and free-trade agreements between partners of the European Union. The parties have set 2010 as the target date for the gradual establishment of this area which will cover most trade with due observance of the obligations resulting from the WTO.

With a view to developing gradual free trade in this area: tariff and non-tariff barriers to trade in manufactured products will be progressively eliminated in accordance with timetables to be negotiated between the partners; taking as a starting point traditional trade flows, and as far as the various agricultural policies allow and with due respect to the results achieved within the GATT negotiations, trade in agricultural products will be progressively liberalized through reciprocal preferential access among the parties; trade in services including right of establishment will be progressively liberalized having due regard to the GATS agreement.

The participants decide to facilitate the progressive establishment of this free-trade area through

- the adoption of suitable measures as regard rules of origin, certification, protection of intellectual and industrial property rights and competition;

- the pursuit and the development of policies based on the principles of market economy and the integration of their economies taking into account their respective needs and levels of development;

- the adjustment and modernization of economic and social structures, giving priority to the promotion and development of the private sector, to the upgrading of the productive sector and to the establishment of an appropriate institutional and regulatory framework for a market economy. They will likewise endeavour to mitigate the negative social consequences which may result from this adjustment, by promoting programmes for the benefit of the neediest populations;

- the promotion of mechanisms to foster transfers of technology.

B) ECONOMIC COOPERATION AND CONCERTED ACTION

Cooperation will be developed in particular in the areas listed below and in this respect the participants:

acknowledge that economic development must be supported both by internal savings, the basis of investment, and by direct foreign investment. They stress the importance of creating an environment conducive to investment, in particular by the progressive elimination of obstacles to such investment which could lead to the transfer of technology and increase production and exports;

affirm that regional cooperation on a voluntary basis, particularly with a view to developing trade between the partners themselves, is a key factor in promoting the creation of a free-trade area;

encourage enterprises to enter into agreements with each other and undertake to promote such cooperation and industrial modernization by providing a favourable environment and regulatory framework. They consider it necessary to adopt and to implement a technical support programme for SMEs;

emphasize their interdependence with regard to the environment, which necessitates a regional approach and increased cooperation, as well as better coordination of existing multilateral programmes, while confirming their attachment to the Barcelona Convention and the Mediterranean Action Plan. They recognize the importance of reconciling economic development with environmental protection, of integrating environmental concerns into the relevant aspects of economic policy and of mitigating the negative environmental consequences which might result. They undertake to establish a short and medium-term priority action programme, including in connection with combating desertification, and to concentrate appropriate technical and financial support on those actions;

recognize the key role of women in development and undertake to promote their active participation in economic and social life and in the creation of employment;

stress the importance of the conservation and rational management of fish stocks and of the improvement of cooperation on research into stocks, including aquaculture, and undertake to facilitate scientific training and research and to envisage creating joint instruments;

acknowledge the pivotal role of the energy sector in the economic Euro-Mediterranean partnership and decide to strengthen cooperation and intensify dialogue in the field of energy policies. They also decide to create the appropriate framework conditions for investments and the activities of energy companies, cooperating in creating the conditions enabling such companies to extend energy networks and promote link-ups;

recognize that water supply together with suitable management and development of resources are priority issues for all Mediterranean partners and that cooperation should be developed in these areas;

agree to cooperate in modernizing and restructuring agriculture and in promoting integrated rural development. This cooperation will focus in particular on technical assistance and training, on support for policies implemented by the partners to diversify production, on the reduction of food dependency and on the promotion of environment-friendly agriculture. They also agree to cooperate in the eradication of illicit crops and the development of any regions affected.

The participants also agree to cooperate in other areas and, to that effect:

stress the importance of developing and improving infrastructures, including through the establishment of an efficient transport system, the development of information technologies and the modernization of telecommunications. They agree to draw up a programme of priorities for that purpose;

undertake to respect the principles of international maritime law, in particular freedom to provide services in international transport and free access to international cargoes. The results of the ongoing multilateral trade negotiations on maritime transport services being conducted within the WTO will be taken into account when agreed;

undertake to encourage cooperation between local authorities and in support of regional planning;

recognizing that science and technology have a significant influence on socio-economic development, agree to strengthen scientific research capacity and development, contribute to the training of scientific and technical staff and promote participation in joint research projects based on the creation of scientific networks;

agree to promote cooperation on statistics in order to harmonize methods and exchange data.

c) FINANCIAL COOPERATION

The participants consider that the creation of a free-trade area and the success of the Euro-Mediterranean partnership require a substantial increase in financial assistance, which must above all encourage sustainable indigenous development and the mobilization of local economic operators. They note in this connection that:

the Cannes European Council agreed to set aside ECU 4 685 million for this financial assistance in the form of available Community budget funds for the period 1995–1999. This will be supplemented by EIB assistance in the form of increased loans and the bilateral financial contributions from the Member States;

effective financial cooperation managed in the framework of a multiannual programme, taking into account the special characteristics of each of the partners is necessary;

sound macro-economic management is of fundamental importance in ensuring the success of the partnership. To this end they agree to promote dialogue on their respective economic policies and on the method of optimizing financial cooperation.

Partnership in Social, Cultural and Human Affairs: Developing Human Resources, Promoting Understanding between Cultures and Exchanges between Civil Societies

The participants recognize that the traditions of culture and civilization throughout the Mediterranean region, dialogue between these cultures and exchanges at human, scientific and technological level are an essential factor in bringing their peoples closer, promoting understanding between them and improving their perception of each other.

In this spirit, the participants agree to establish a partnership in social, cultural and human affairs. To this end:

they reaffirm that dialogue and respect between cultures and religions are a necessary pre-condition for bringing the peoples closer. In this connection they stress the importance of the role the mass media can play in the reciprocal recognition and understanding of cultures as a source of mutual enrichment;

they stress the essential nature of the development of human resources, both as regards the education and training of young people in particular and in the area of culture. They express their intent to promote cultural exchanges and knowledge of other languages, respecting the cultural identity of each partner, and to implement a lasting policy of educational and cultural programmes; in this context, the partners undertake to adopt measures to facilitate human exchanges, in particular by improving administrative procedures;

they underline the importance of the health sector for sustainable development and express their intention of promoting the effective participation of the community in operations to improve health and well-being;

they recognize the importance of social development which, in their view, must go hand in hand with any economic development. They attach particular importance to respect for fundamental social rights, including the right to development;

they recognize the essential contribution civil society can make in the process of development of the Euro-Mediterranean partnership and as an essential factor for greater understanding and closeness between peoples;

they accordingly agree to strengthen and/or introduce the necessary instruments of decentralized cooperation to encourage exchanges between those active in development within the framework of national laws: leaders of political and civil society, the cultural and religious world, universities, the research community, the media, organizations, the trade unions and public and private enterprises;

on this basis, they recognize the importance of encouraging contacts and exchanges between young people in the context of programmes for decentralized cooperation;

they will encourage actions of support for democratic institutions and for the strengthening of the rule of law and civil society;

they recognize that current population trends represent a priority challenge which must be counterbalanced by appropriate policies to accelerate economic take-off;

they acknowledge the importance of the role played by migration in their relationships. They agree to strengthen their cooperation to reduce migratory pressures, among other things through vocational training programmes and programmes of assistance for job creation. They undertake to guarantee protection of all the rights recognized under existing legislation of migrants legally resident in their respective territories;

in the area of illegal immigration they decide to establish closer cooperation. In this context, the partners, aware of their responsibility for readmission, agree to adopt the relevant provisions and measures, by means of bilateral agreements or arrangements, in order to readmit their nationals who are in an illegal situation. To that end, the Member States of the European Union take citizens to mean nationals of the Member States, as defined for Community purposes;

they agree to strengthen cooperation by means of various measures to prevent terrorism and fight it more effectively together;

by the same token they consider it necessary to fight jointly and effectively against drug trafficking, international crime and corruption;

they underline the importance of waging a determined campaign against racism, xenophobia and intolerance and agree to cooperate to that end.

Follow-up to the Conference

The participants:

considering that the Barcelona Conference provides the basis for a process, which is open and should develop;

reaffirming their will to establish a partnership based on the principles and objectives defined in this Declaration;

resolved to give practical expression to this Euro-Mediterranean partnership;

convinced that, in order to achieve this objective, it is necessary to continue the comprehensive dialogue thus initiated and to carry out a series of specific actions;

hereby adopt the attached work programme:

The Ministers for Foreign Affairs will meet periodically in order to monitor the application of this Declaration and define actions enabling the objectives of the partnership to be achieved.

The various activities will be followed by ad hoc thematic meetings of ministers, senior officials and experts, exchanges of experience and information, contacts between those active in civil society and by any other appropriate means.

Contacts between parliamentarians, regional authorities, local authorities and the social partners will be encouraged.

A "Euro-Mediterranean Committee for the Barcelona process" at senior-official level, consisting of the European Union Troïka and one representative of each Mediterranean partner, will hold regular meetings to prepare the meeting of the Ministers for Foreign Affairs, take stock of and evaluate the follow-up to the Barcelona process and all its components and update the work programme.

Appropriate preparatory and follow-up work for the meetings resulting from the Barcelona work programme and from the conclusions of the "Euro-Mediterranean Committee for the Barcelona process" will be undertaken by the Commission departments.

The next meeting of the Ministers for Foreign Affairs will be held in the first semester of 1997 in one of the twelve Mediterranean partners of the European Union, to be determined through further consultations.

Annex

Work Programme

I. Introduction

The aim of this programme is to implement the objectives of the Barcelona Declaration, and to respect its principles, through regional and multilateral actions. It is complementary both to the bilateral cooperation, implemented in particular under the agreements between the EU and its Mediterranean partners, and to the cooperation already existing in other multilateral fora.

The preparation and the follow-up to the various actions will be implemented in accordance with the principles and mechanisms set out in the Barcelona Declaration.

The priority actions for further cooperation are listed below. This does not exclude Euro-Mediterranean cooperation being extended to other actions if the partners so agree.

The actions may apply to States, their local and regional authorities as well as actors of their civil society.

With the agreement of the participants, other countries or organizations may be involved in the actions contained in the work programme. The implementation must take place in a flexible and transparent way.

With the agreement of the participants, future Euro-Mediterranean cooperation
will take account, as appropriate, of the opinions and recommendations resulting from the relevant discussions held at various levels in the region.

The implementation of the programme should start as soon as practical after the
Barcelona Conference. It will be reviewed at the next Euro-Mediterranean
Conference on the basis of a report to be prepared by the European Commis-
sion departments, particularly on the basis of reports from the various meet-
ings and Groups mentioned below, and approved by the "Euro-Mediterranean
Committee for the Barcelona process" set up by the Barcelona Declaration.

II. Political and Security Partnership: Establishing a common area of peace and stability

With a view to contributing to the objective of progressively creating a zone of
peace, stability and security in the Mediterranean, senior officials will meet periodically, starting within the first quarter of 1996. They will:

– conduct a political dialogue to examine the most appropriate means and
   methods of implementing the principles adopted by the Barcelona Declaration, and

– submit practical proposals in due time for the next Euro-Mediterranean
   Meeting of Foreign Ministers.

Foreign policy institutes in the Euro-Mediterranean region will be encouraged to
establish a network for more intensive cooperation which could become oper-
ational as of 1996.

III. Economic and Financial Partnership: Building a zone of shared prosperity

Meetings will take place periodically at the level of Ministers, officials or experts, as
appropriate, to promote cooperation in the following areas. These meetings
may be supplemented, where appropriate, by conferences or seminars involving the private sector likewise.

ESTABLISHMENT OF A EURO-MEDITERRANEAN FREE TRADE AREA

The establishment of a free trade area in accordance with the principles contained
in the Barcelona Declaration is an essential element of the Euro-Mediterranean partnership.

Cooperation will focus on practical measures to facilitate the establishment of free
trade as well as its consequences, including:

– harmonizing rules and procedures in the customs field, with a view in particular to the progressive introduction of cumulation of origin; in the mean-
   time, favourable consideration will be given, where appropriate, to finding
   ad hoc solutions in particular cases;

- harmonization of standards, including meetings arranged by the European Standards Organisations;

- elimination of unwarranted technical barriers to trade in agricultural products and adoption of relevant measures related to plant-health and veterinary rules as well as other legislation on foodstuffs;

- cooperation among statistics organizations with a view to providing reliable data on a harmonized basis;

- possibilities for regional and subregional cooperation (without prejudice to initiatives taken in other existing fora).

INVESTMENT

The object of cooperation will be to help create a climate favourable to the removal of obstacles to investment, by giving greater thought to the definition of such obstacles and to means, including in the banking sector, of promoting such investment.

INDUSTRY

Industrial modernisation and increased competitiveness will be key factors for the success of the Euro-Mediterranean partnership. In this context, the private sector will play a more important role in the economic development of the region and the creation of employment. Cooperation will focus on:

- the adaptation of the industrial fabric to the changing international environment, in particular to the emergence of the information society;

- the framework for and the preparation of the modernisation and restructuring of existing enterprises, especially in the public sector, including privatisation;

- the use of international or European standards and the upgrading of conformity testing, certification, accreditation and quality standards.

Particular attention will be paid to means of encouraging cooperation among SMEs and creating the conditions for their development, including the possibility of organising workshops, taking account of experience acquired under MED-INVEST and inside the European Union.

AGRICULTURE

While pointing out that such matters are covered under bilateral relations in the main, cooperation in this area will focus on:

- support for policies implemented by them to diversify production;

- reduction of food dependency;

- promotion of environment-friendly agriculture;

- closer relations between businesses, groups and organizations representing trades and professions in the partner States on a voluntary basis;

–support for privatization;

–technical assistance and training;

–harmonization of plant-health and veterinary standards;

–integrated rural development, including improvement of basic services and the development of associated economic activities;

–cooperation among rural regions, exchange of experience and know-how concerning rural development;

–development of regions affected by the eradication of illicit crops.

TRANSPORT

Efficient interoperable transport links between the EU and its Mediterranean partners, and among the partners themselves, as well as free access to the market for services in international maritime transport, are essential to the development of trade patterns and the smooth operation of the Euro-Mediterranean partnership.

The Transport Ministers of Western Mediterranean countries met twice in 1995 and, following the Regional Conference for the Development of Maritime Transport in the Mediterranean, the Mediterranean Waterborne Transport Working Group adopted a multiannual programme.

Cooperation will focus on:

–development of an efficient Trans-Mediterranean multimodal combined sea and air transport system, through the improvement and modernization of ports and airports, the suppression of unwarranted restrictions, the simplification of procedures, the improvement of maritime and air safety, the harmonization of environmental standards at a high level including more efficient monitoring of maritime pollution, and the development of harmonized traffic management systems;

–development of east–west land links on the southern and eastern shores of the Mediterranean, and

–connection of Mediterranean transport networks to the Trans-European Network in order to ensure their interoperability.

ENERGY

A high-level Conference was held in Tunisia in 1995 with a follow-up meeting in Athens and an Energy Conference in Madrid on 20 November 1995.

With a view to creating appropriate conditions for investment in and activities by energy companies, future cooperation will focus, inter alia on:

–fostering the association of Mediterranean countries with the Treaty on the European Energy Charter;

–energy planning;

-encouraging producer–consumer dialogue;

-oil and gas exploration, refining, transportation, distribution, and regional and trans-regional trade;

-coal production and handling;

-generation and transmission of power and interconnection and development of networks;

-energy efficiency;

-new and renewable sources of energy;

-energy-related environmental issues;

-development of joint research programmes;

-training and information activities in the energy sector.

Telecommunications and information technology

With a view to developing a modern, efficient telecommunications network, cooperation will focus on:

-information and telecommunications infrastructures (minimum regulatory framework, standards, conformity testing, network interoperability, etc.);

-regional infrastructures including links with European networks;

-access to services, and

-new services in priority fields of application.

Intensification of Euro-Mediterranean exchanges and access to the nascent information society will be facilitated by more efficient information and communications infrastructures.

A regional conference is planned for 1996 with the aim of paving the way for pilot projects to show the concrete benefits of the information society.

Regional planning

Cooperation will focus on:

-defining a regional planning strategy for the Euro-Mediterranean area commensurate with the countries' requirements and special features;

-promoting cross-border cooperation in areas of mutual interest.

Tourism

The Ministers for Tourism, meeting in Casablanca, adopted the Mediterranean Tourism Charter in 1995. The cooperation actions to be initiated will relate in particular to information, promotion and training.

Environment

Cooperation will focus on:

—assessing environmental problems in the Mediterranean region and defining, where appropriate, the initiatives to be taken;

—making proposals to establish and subsequently update a short and medium-term priority environmental action programme for intervention coordinated by the European Commission and supplemented by long-term actions; it should include among the main areas for action, the following: integrated management of water, soil and coastal areas; management of waste; preventing and combating air pollution and pollution in the Mediterranean sea; natural heritage, landscapes and site conservation and management; Mediterranean forest protection, conservation and restoration, in particular through the prevention and control of erosion, soil degradation, forest fires and combating desertification; transfer of Community experience in financing techniques, legislation and environmental monitoring; integration of environmental concerns in all policies;

—setting up a regular dialogue to monitor the implementation of the action programme;

—reinforcing regional and subregional cooperation and strengthening coordination with the Mediterranean Action Plan;

—stimulating coordination of investments from various sources, and implementation of relevant international conventions;

—promoting the adoption and implementation of legislation and regulatory measures when required, especially preventive measures and appropriate high standards.

SCIENCE AND TECHNOLOGY

Cooperation will focus on:

—promoting research and development and tackling the problem of the widening gap in scientific achievement, taking account of the principle of mutual advantage;

—stepping up exchanges of experience in the scientific sectors and policies which might best enable the Mediterranean partners to reduce the gap between them and their European neighbours and to promote the transfer of technology.

—helping train scientific and technical staff by increasing participation in joint research projects.

Following the Ministerial meeting at Sophia Antipolis in March 1995, a Monitoring Committee was set up; this Committee will meet for the first time immediately after the Barcelona Conference. It will focus on making recommendations for the joint implementation of the policy priorities agreed at Ministerial level.

Water

The Mediterranean Water Charter was adopted in Rome in 1992.

Water is a priority issue for all the Mediterranean partners and will gain in importance as water scarcity becomes more pressing. The purpose of cooperation in this area will be as follows:

- to take stock of the situation taking into account current and future needs;

- to identify ways of reinforcing regional cooperation;

- to make proposals for rationalising the planning and management of water resources, where appropriate on a joint basis;

- to contribute towards the creation of new sources of water.

Fisheries

In view of the importance of conservation and rational management of Mediterranean fish stocks, cooperation in the framework of the General Fisheries Council for the Mediterranean will be reinforced.

Following the Ministerial Fisheries Conference held in Heraklion in 1994, appropriate follow-up action will be taken in the legal sphere through meetings to take place in 1996.

Cooperation will be improved on research into fish stocks, including aquaculture, as well as into training and scientific research.

IV. Partnership in Social, Cultural and Human Affairs: Developing human resources, promoting understanding between cultures and exchanges between civil societies

Development of human resources

The Euro-Mediterranean partnership must contribute to enhancing educational levels throughout the region, whilst laying special emphasis on the Mediterranean partners. To this end, a regular dialogue on educational policies will take place, initially focusing on vocational training, technology in education, the universities and other higher-education establishments and research. In this context as well as in other areas, particular attention will be paid to the role of women. The Euro-Arab Business School in Granada and the European Foundation in Turin will also contribute to this cooperation.

A meeting of representatives of the vocational training sector (policy makers, academics, trainers, etc) will be organised with the aim of sharing modern management approaches.

A meeting will be held of representatives of universities and higher-education establishments. The European Commission will strengthen its ongoing MED-Campus programme.

A meeting will also be called on the subject of technology in education.

MUNICIPALITIES AND REGIONS

Municipalities and regional authorities need to be closely involved in the operation of the Euro-Mediterranean Partnership. City and regional representatives will be encouraged to meet each year to take stock of their common challenges and exchange experiences. This will be organised by the European Commission and will take account of previous experience.

DIALOGUE BETWEEN CULTURES AND CIVILIZATIONS

Given the importance of improving mutual understanding by promoting cultural exchanges and knowledge of languages, officials and experts will meet in order to make concrete proposals for action, inter alia, in the following fields: cultural and creative heritage, cultural and artistic events, co-productions (theatre and cinema), translations and other means of cultural dissemination, training.

Greater understanding among the major religions present in the Euro-Mediterranean region will facilitate greater mutual tolerance and cooperation. Support will be given to periodic meetings of representatives of religions and religious institutions as well as theologians, academics and others concerned, with the aim of breaking down prejudice, ignorance and fanaticism and fostering cooperation at grass-roots level. The conferences held in Stockholm (15/17.6.1995) and Toledo (4/7.11.1995) may serve as examples in this context.

MEDIA

Close interaction between the media will work in favour of better cultural understanding. The European Union will actively promote such interaction, in particular through the ongoing MED-Media programme. An annual meeting of representatives of the media will be organised in this context.

YOUTH

Youth exchanges should be the means to prepare future generations for a closer cooperation between the Euro-Mediterranean partners. A Euro-Mediterranean youth exchange programme should therefore be established based on experience acquired in Europe and taking account of the partners' needs; this programme should take account of the importance of vocational training, particularly for those without qualifications, and of the training of organizers and social workers in the youth field. The European Commission will make the necessary proposals before the next meeting of Euro-Mediterranean Foreign Ministers.

EXCHANGES BETWEEN CIVIL SOCIETIES

Senior officials will meet periodically to discuss measures likely to facilitate human exchanges resulting from the Euro-Mediterranean partnership, especially those involving officials, scientists, academics, businessmen, students and sportsmen, including the improvement and simplification of administrative procedures, particularly where unnecessary administrative obstacles might exist.

Social development

The Euro-Mediterranean partnership must contribute to improving the living and working conditions and increasing the employment level of the population in the Mediterranean partner States, in particular of women and the neediest strata of the population. In this context the partners attach particular importance to the respect and promotion of basic social rights. To that end, actors in social policies will meet periodically at the appropriate level.

Health

The partners agree to concentrate cooperation in this area on:

–action on raising awareness, information and prevention;

–development of public health services, in particular health care, primary health centres, maternal and child health care services, family planning, epidemiological supervision systems and measures to control communicable diseases;

–training of health and health-administration personnel;

–medical cooperation in the event of natural disasters.

Migration

Given the importance of the issue of migration for Euro-Mediterranean relations, meetings will be encouraged in order to make proposals concerning migration flows and pressures. These meetings will take account of experience acquired, inter alia, under the MED-Migration programme, particularly as regards improving the living conditions of migrants legally established in the Union.

Terrorism, Drug trafficking, Organised crime

Fighting terrorism will have to be a priority for all the parties. To that end, officials will meet periodically with the aim of strengthening cooperation among police, judicial and other authorities. In this context, consideration will be given, in particular, to stepping up exchanges of information and improving extradition procedures.

Officials will meet periodically to discuss practical measures which can be taken to improve cooperation among police, judicial, customs, administrative and other authorities in order to combat, in particular, drug trafficking and organised crime, including smuggling.

All these meetings will be organized with due regard for the need for a differentiated approach that takes into account the diversity of the situation in each country.

Illegal immigration

Officials will meet periodically to discuss practical measures which can be taken to improve cooperation among police, judicial, customs, administrative and other authorities in order to combat illegal immigration.

These meetings will be organized with due regard for the need for a differentiated approach that takes into account the diversity of the situation in each country.

V. Institutional Contacts

EURO-MEDITERRANEAN PARLIAMENTARY DIALOGUE

An Inter-Parliamentary Conference on Security and Cooperation in the Mediterranean was held in Valletta from 1 to 4 November 1995. The European Parliament is invited to take the initiative with other parliaments concerning the future Euro-Mediterranean Parliamentary Dialogue, which could enable the elected representatives of the partners to exchange ideas on a wide range of issues.

OTHER INSTITUTIONAL CONTACTS

Regular contacts among other European organs, in particular the Economic and Social Committee of the European Community, and their Mediterranean counterparts, would contribute to a better understanding of the major issues relevant in the Euro-Mediterranean partnership.

To this end, the Economic and Social Committee is invited to take the initiative in establishing links with its Mediterranean counterparts and equivalent bodies. In this context, a Euro-Mediterranean meeting of Economic and Social Committees and equivalent bodies will take place in Madrid on 12 and 13 December.

About the Author

Dr. William H. Lewis is an adjunct fellow of the CSIS Preventive Diplomacy Program. He is a recognized authority on greater Middle East political–military issues. For a number of years, he served as regional affairs specialist in the U.S. Department of State and as a member of the Policy Planning Staff of the secretary of defense. In the latter capacity, he led special missions in the Middle East and Africa and served on presidential task forces. Dr. Lewis has held faculty appointments at the University of Michigan, Georgetown University, and the Johns Hopkins University.